YOUTH AND DISABILITY

Interdisciplinary Disability Studies

Series Editor:
Mark Sherry, The University of Toledo, USA

Disability studies has made great strides in exploring power and the body. This series extends the interdisciplinary dialogue between disability studies and other fields by asking how disability studies can influence a particular field. It will show how a deep engagement with disability studies changes our understanding of the following fields: sociology, literary studies, gender studies, bioethics, social work, law, education, and history. This ground-breaking series identifies both the practical and theoretical implications of such an interdisciplinary dialogue and challenges people in disability studies as well as other disciplinary fields to critically reflect on their professional praxis in terms of theory, practice, and methods.

Youth and Disability

A Challenge to Mr Reasonable

JENNY SLATER
Sheffield Hallam University, UK

ASHGATE

Published by
Ashgate Publishing Limited
Wey Court East
Union Road
Farnham
Surrey, GU9 7PT
England

Ashgate Publishing Company
110 Cherry Street
Suite 3-1
Burlington, VT 05401-3818
USA

www.ashgate.com

British Library Cataloguing in Publication Data
A catalogue record for this book is available from the British Library

The Library of Congress has cataloged the printed edition as follows:
Slater, Jenny.
  Youth and disability a challenge to Mr Reasonable / by Jenny Slater.
    pages cm. -- (Interdisciplinary disability studies)
  Includes bibliographical references and index.
  ISBN 978-1-4724-2851-6 (hardback) -- ISBN 978-1-4724-2852-3 (ebook) -- ISBN 978-1-4724-2853-0 (epub) 1. Youth with disabilities. 2. Sociology of disability--Research. I. Title.
  HV1569.3.Y68S583 2015
  305.9'080835--dc23

2014037361

ISBN 9781472428516 (hbk)
ISBN 9781472428523 (ebk – PDF)
ISBN 9781472428530 (ebk – ePUB)

MIX
Paper from
responsible sources
FSC
www.fsc.org
FSC® C013985

Printed in the United Kingdom by Henry Ling Limited, at the Dorset Press, Dorchester, DT1 1HD

Contents

List of Figures

About the Author

Dr Jenny Slater is currently a lecturer within the Sheffield Institute of Education (SIoE) at Sheffield Hallam University (SHU). She teaches across courses within the Education Studies programme, specialising in disability studies and social justice modules which explore cultures of in/exclusion within education. Her research explores youth and disability as socio-cultural and political constructs. Although focusing on 'youth' and 'disability' her research is interdisciplinary and intersectional; with a particular focus on gender and sexuality. Her latest research interest is in how toilets function as socio-cultural spaces within the lives of young people. She is co-organiser of the *Disability Research Forum* (DRF); a monthly forum discussing disability (and related) research held at SHU. She is part of the organising committee for the *Theorising Normalcy and the Mundane* conference series.

Acknowledgements

The story of this book is only ever partial, and always connected. This means that there are lots of people I need to thank.

Firstly, I am grateful to Ashgate for publishing this book, particularly Claire for her patient responses to my questions, and Mark, for his careful reading and thoughtful responses. I also have to thank the young disabled people and their allies who shared their thoughts, feelings and creativity around 'youth' and 'disability'; as well as staff working within the organisations where I spent time. I extend an especially big thank you to Freyja and Embla. What I have learnt from these young women is immeasurable; they have made me see the world differently.

I thank my academic and activist comrades: my students that have challenged my thinking; those that responded to my Facebook 'peer-review' call, took time to read my chapters and gave me much appreciated feedback; people that have made me feel so at home in the world of disability studies: members of the *Disability Research Forum* in Sheffield; the *Centre of Disability Studies* at the University of Iceland; and (particularly) to the regular cohort at *Theorising Normalcy and the Mundane*. Special mention to my buddies: China Mills, Anat Greenstein, Steve Graby, Jon Harvey and Cassie Ogden – thinking/drinking/ laughing/eating with you lot could never happen enough. Thanks of course to Katherine Runswick-Cole (AKA KRC: academic-life-advisor), and my PhD supervisors, Dan Goodley and Rebecca Lawthom. Dan, thank you for guiding me, giving me confidence, and encouraging me to wander into places I never thought I'd go … but also for making my time at MMU a lot of fun.

These are all people and arenas I would not have discovered without my undergraduate tutor, colleague, and friend, Rebecca Mallett (the one who taught me everything I know). For this, Rebecca, I will always be grateful.

I've a huge amount of gratitude to pay to my brilliant friends and family who have put up with me/put the world to rights with me during both my PhD and this book-writing process. Thanks Sarah, for looking after me and indulging my whisky-drinking whims; Siân, for the trips over the Pennines when a pint was called for; and Jóna and Bjarni, my Icelandic Mum and Dad. To Em: thanks for not being annoyed when I was flaky, but even more: thanks for thinking so hard about the world, for the conversations, for what you've taught me, and for everything else.

To Mum, Dad, Bob, Jim, Dan, Uncle A and Steph: well, you're just ace. xxxxxxxxxxxx

List of Abbreviations

CDS	Critical Disability Studies
IL	Independent Living
ILC	Independent Living Centre
ILM	Independent Living Movement
LGBT*	Lesbian, Gay, Bisexual and Trans*. The asterisk (*) in trans* is used to represent all non cisgender identities. Including, for example, gender queer and non-binary people, as well as trans men and trans women. The asterisk in LGBT* also signifies other diversities of genders and sexualities within queer culture, such as intersex and asexual people.
PA	Personal Assistant
YF	Youth Forum

Introduction
Theoretical Perspectives

Dear Mr Reasonable

This book begins with an opening letter to somebody you will come to know as Mr Reasonable.

Dear Mr Reasonable,

As I try to keep you at a distance, you're probably surprised to hear from me. Well, I'm addressing this book to you, Mr Reasonable, because the time has come for us to have a chat. This is a book about conducting research at the intersection of youth and disability. Through a series of essays it aims to challenge a dangerous and pervasive (neo)liberal[1] (Sothern 2007) reasonableness which threatens, amongst others, young disabled people. I'll explain more of what I mean by this, both in this letter and as the book goes on. Before we get started, however, let me remind you of who you are, Mr Reasonable, to let other readers know why I'm aiming this book at you.

What you are not, Mr Reasonable, is the *overtly* nasty person that it's easy to be angry with. In fact, you could be that person that I occasionally find myself describing as 'alright really'. You are the creation of systems which prioritise certain ways of being over and above others. By functioning around pervasive, market-driven ideas of what is 'good', 'ideal' and 'normal', these global capitalist systems make your life appear as 'reasonable', whereas the lives of others around you are deemed 'unreasonable'. You are, for example, the Reasonable Careers Advisor who asserted that if I did not 'speak properly', dared to utter an 'erm' or an 'um' in a job interview, I would remain unemployed. You are the Reasonable Academic who told me this was 'just the way it is' when the ableism of that careers advice was pointed out. You are the Reasonable Manager that told my friend that she needed to 'man up and grow some balls' in order to survive work in the public sector: the workplace will not change to accommodate you, so you must change to accommodate it. You're the Reasonable Landlord, the Reasonable Councillor and the Reasonable Politician that live dogmatically by the reasonable, bureaucratic rules of Western (neo)liberal individualism

---

1   I explain the term *(neo)liberal* further in Chapter 1.

(Titchkosky 2011). As we'll see in Chapter 1, in current political times, the cries to 'be reasonable – we have to draw the line somewhere!' are heard more loudly, and more harmfully, than ever (Titchkosky 2012).

Yet, although you may be a creation of systems, Mr Reasonable, I argue in this book that your discourse of reasonableness works to maintain the status quo. You attempt (though, I would argue, inevitably fail) to be what Garland-Thomson (2002: 10) calls the 'normate', 'the corporeal incarnation of culture's collective, unmarked, normative characteristics'. Through aiming to embody normativity you perpetuate a pervasive discourse of ableism, a 'network of beliefs, processes and practices that produces a particular kind of self and body (the corporeal standard) that is projected as the perfect, species-typical and therefore essential and fully human' (Fiona Kumari Campbell 2009: 44). This ableist 'fully human' corporeal standard is not only reliant upon the category of disability. Rather '[t]he nuances of ableism […] are transcategorical, having specific cultural alignments with other factors such as race, gender, sexuality and coloniality' (Fiona Kumari Campbell 2012: 214). Through unquestionably attempting to be the normate, you make reasonable the marginalisation and oppression of those who do not/cannot/will not conform.

I address this book to you then Mr Reasonable, as the guardian of a dangerously reasonable textbook of (neo)liberalism. I'll argue that this textbook makes both 'adulthood' and 'ability' 'reasonable', but by doing this marks 'youth' and 'disability' as their unreasonable Others. Furthermore, we'll see that all are discursive concepts entwined and implicated with constructions of race, class, gender, sexuality, and so on. You, Mr Reasonable, therefore serve as a metaphor to illustrate the failures of the normative imagination. The pervasive implicitness of this normative imagination means we all, myself included, have bits of Mr Reasonable residing within us. This book engages with 'youth' and 'disability' as socially and culturally constituted categories to ask what purpose 'the reasonable' serves in all our lives.

Let us learn together, Mr Reasonable.

Love from,

Jen x

Youth and Disability: A Challenge to the Reasonable

This book sits at the intersection of 'youth' and 'disability'. The stories shared aim to challenge the normative imaginary of what it is to embody 'youth' and 'disability'. Importantly, however, they also aim to rethink ableist, adultist and *reasonable* rhetoric, which, I'll argue, results in only some lives qualifying as intelligible, liveable, and fully human. The book is, therefore, about more than just young disabled people. Critical disability studies (CDS, which is introduced further as this chapter goes on) is my guiding tool to think intersectionally about the multitudes of other identities with which 'youth' and 'disability' intertwine.

This is not to say, however, that young disabled people do not occupy an important position within the text. 'Imagining otherwise' about 'youth' and 'disability' and so on is done as we explore issues of subjectivity, resistance and survival that were told to me through a 12-month long ethnography in the UK and Iceland. Through outlining my method/ology, this chapter introduces both the theoretical tools that will equip us for the rest of the book, and also the fieldwork – which I deem 'unreasonable', 'fantastical' and 'utopian'. The arguments made throughout are influenced by the ambiguity and questioning of queer theory. This chapter draws on Gibson-Graham's (1999) term 'queer(y)ing' to outline how an approach that continually queer(y)s ethnography, the process of academic writing, myself, and finally, ethics, leads to the auto/ethnographic, reflexive approach taken in this book. In the final section of this chapter I explain the flow and structure of the book. I begin, however, with a definition of disability (or not).

Defining Disability (or Not)

The first thing to ask when I claim a CDS approach is what I mean by 'disability'. British disability studies rests upon foundations carved by the Union of the Physically Impaired Against Segregation (UPIAS) and the development of the British social model of disability. The social model of disability separated impairment – a perceived lack of or difference in bodily function – from disability and societal barriers, be these physical or attitudinal, which hinder the lives of disabled people (Oliver 1990). This was a radical step in disability politics. The 'problem' of disability was removed from disabled people and considered as the product of unequal economic market relations. The social model gave disabled people the language to shift disability from a medicalised problem residing within an individual, to a problem of societal injustice. To be a disabled person was to be a person with an impairment who was disabled by society. Disability was hence made an identity on which to base politics, and thus brought into the world of identity politics (Davis 2002). British disability studies grew up alongside this identity politics and activism. The gains made by disabled people through the separation of impairment and disability should not be underestimated. I celebrate these political gains, and believe the social model remains a radical tool in disability politics and activism.

For my project, however, a social model definition of disability which considers disability purely as based within society and outside the body is not always useful. Firstly, it reifies the 'fact' of impairment. To be a 'disabled person' is to have restrictions placed upon one by a society that devalues people with impairments; yet, the impairment remains as 'fact' (Hughes and Paterson 1997). Secondly, attention is shifted away from the body. Feminist critiques have problematised talk of the body being restricted within disability studies (Crow 2012; Morris 1992, 1998; Thomas 1999). Shifting the attention away from the body in the early days of disability politics was done for good reason. Previous medical focus constructed the disabled body as deficient, in need of intervention, rehabilitation and, ultimately, extermination. Therefore, to remove the gaze from the disabled body, and challenge a disabling society was key to the political struggle of disabled people. Yet the body and issues of embodiment are important to my research, especially due to their prevalence in discourses surrounding youth (Featherstone 1982; Slater 2012).

As disability studies evolved, so did approaches to discuss 'the body' within it. Some have taken a critical realist perspective to talk about the body (Shakespeare 2006; Shakespeare and Watson 2001). Critical realists maintain the 'brute fact' of impairment as biological limitation and assume the reality of a body untouched by culture (Goodley and Runswick-Cole 2012). Sitting with the Nordic Relational Model of disability (Tøssebro 2004), critical realists see disability as a relational concept between 'really' impaired bodies and socio-cultural environments; the mismatch of which restricts possibility (Shakespeare 2006). Neither, however, do I find this conception useful. Although it means the body can enter conversation, it maintains the reality of impairment and removes bodies from discourse and culture (Goodley and Runswick-Cole 2012). Both social model and critical realist perspectives create disabled/non-disabled dualities which, although sometimes useful in delivering a particular message, are not always helpful to my work (Tregaskis and Goodley 2005).

Hughes and Paterson (1997), on the other hand, call for a sociology of impairment. Drawing on post-structuralism, they argue that we need to consider impairment and the body as part of, rather than separate from, socio-cultural discourse. We can take pain as an example of this[2] (Mallett and Runswick-Cole 2014). Staunch social model perspectives have been criticised for not leaving space for discussions of pain (Crow 2012). Critical realist perspectives, on the other hand, do discuss pain (Shakespeare 2006), but see pain as something that the body experiences outside of society and culture; an unpleasant feeling to signal that attention is needed (i.e. stop doing that). Sociologies of impairment, however, would consider how pain is understood and experienced differently dependent on the cultural and social contexts of a specific time and place. To give just one example, although pain is often thought to be something to be avoided, some people actively seek out pain through sadomasochism

---

2   For a more detailed theorisation of pain see Chapter 8 of Mallett and Runswick-Cole (2014).

or processes of body modification (Mallett and Runswick-Cole 2014). Research in disability studies concerning experiences of impairment and pain, includes Sheppard's (2014) work, which explores the narratives of people with chronic pain who also use pain within their erotic activities.

Theorisations exploring both impairment (perceived bodily differences) and disability (social oppression based on these differences) as socially and culturally constituted resonate in this book. Without denying the lived-reality of 'being disabled', or indeed 'young', which I will come onto shortly, this book is about questioning the meanings we give to things, and how this constricts what people can do and be. I consciously use the term 'disability' ambiguously and situate my work within CDS. As Goodley (2011: 157) writes: 'while critical disability studies may start with disability, they never end with it'. CDS is an interdisciplinary theoretical endeavour that seeks to capture and interpret the lived experience of disability whilst disturbing traditional conceptions of dis/ability and difference more widely (Fiona Kumari Campbell 2009; Goodley 2011). I use the term dis/ability here to contest implicit assumptions of a disabled/able duality. There are times within the text, however, when I will refer to 'disability' or 'ability'. When I refer to 'disability' I am speaking of a political identity (Mallett and Slater 2014); and when I write of 'ability', I am referring to an idealised ideology which we are all implicated within. Indeed, Campbell (2009) poses that we step back from the academic discussion of disability, removing the gaze from the disabled body, to instead focus upon the construction of ability. In my musings over youth I remain vigilant to ableism and utilise Campbell's definition of ableism as:

> A network of beliefs, processes and practices that produces a particular kind of self and body (the corporeal standard) that is projected as the perfect, species-typical and therefore essential and fully human. Disability then is cast as a diminished state of being human. (Fiona Kumari Campbell 2009: 44)

I argue in Chapter 2 that the 'able', corporeal standard body is inherently adult. An ableist perspective is an adultist perspective; and an adultist perspective is innately ableist. Ableism and adulthood are therefore integral to any discussions of youth and disability. Furthermore, both are co-constituted by positions of race, gender, sexuality, class (and so on), and situated within transnational capitalism. To consider difference more widely than just disability, CDS demands intersectionality (Goodley 2011). At no point do I stop at an analysis of disability. It is obvious, yet depressingly routinely denied, that disabled young people are also gendered, sexed, raced, and classed beings (Goodley 2011; Priestley 2003). Listening to young disabled participants over Chapters 3–6 shows the importance of taking an intersectional approach: considering the axes of gender, sexuality, race, class, and so on. The stories which were shared with me through research mean my intersectional focus leans particularly towards gender and sexuality; to this end, ableism is considered most fully in Chapter 6 in relation to gender, sexuality and the body.

Rather than defining disability I instead appreciate it as slippery, fluid, heterogeneous and deeply intersectional (Shildrick 2009). To define, Shildrick (2009) argues, is to normalise rather than destabilise the categories we separate human beings into. At the crux of this book is a questioning categorisation: be this in relation to disability, age, or other intersectional categories. By refusing to pin down disability I am neither denying the possibility of either identifying or being constituted as a disabled person, nor the significance of disability in the lives of disabled people, including those whose stories are shared in this book. Post-structural accounts have, at times, been criticised for denying disabled people's subjectivity (Erevelles 2011; Greenstein and Graby 2013). I remain vigilant to this criticism and struggle with issues of subjectivity throughout. I argue that there are infinite different forms of embodiment (Shildrick 2009), which may at times be uncomfortable or painful, but equally, joyful and liberating (Morris 1991). Disability and impairment are relational concepts, mediated by: social, historical, economic, cultural and political factors (Davis 2008; Longmore 2003; Timimi, Gardner and McCabe 2010); time (Chandler 2010; Ferris 2010; Michalko 2010; Slater 2012; Stein 2010; Titchkosky 2010); and space (Hansen and Philo 2007; Titchkosky 2011). Different embodiments alter the way we live in the world but the consequential living is not merely a result of impairment or disability. Numerous factors intersect, influence and bounce off one-another to produce socio-economic and political inequalities (Crenshaw 1989). The way we live is mediated by, yet not restricted to: our embodied physicalities that alter what our bodies can do (Morris 1991; Shildrick 2009); material and environmental factors which prevent or allow us to act in certain ways (Oliver 1990); messages we are delivered through discourse and culture about what we *should* do and be (Reeve 2002) in comparison to 'normal' and favoured ways of living and being (Davis 2010); and our relational agency and autonomy (Greenstein and Graby 2013; Runswick-Cole and Goodley 2013) – all fluid factors that change throughout our lives. We rely on heavily-loaded frames handed to us through discourse and culture to define what we mean by disability (Gergen 2008). As a society, we value some forms of embodiment over others, and have chosen to label some bodies as 'impaired' and gone on to 'disable' these bodies (people) (Davis 2002; Shildrick 2009; Wendell 2010).

If disability is such a slippery concept, how did I do fieldwork with young disabled people? I reiterate that by refusing to pin down disability I am not denying the lived-reality of disability or disabled people's lives. Western societies are constructed around binaries: disabled/non-disabled; man/women;

straight/gay; good/bad; right/wrong. As Shildrick (2009: 3) writes, although 'their power may be based on an illusion, [...] its operation is all too real. What matters is that we do not mistake the challenge to the *effects* of binary opposition as the limit of what is possible and necessary'. We will see as the book goes on, whether or not I believe in an inherent 'truth' of disability, that there is a lived reality of 'being disabled' ('its operation is all too real') and being disabled has consequences ('the *effects* of binary opposition'). However, what this means varies from person to person over time and place: our own dis/abled relationships to and with disability will change throughout our lives (Longmore 2003; Watson 2002). One of the interwoven arguments made in this book is that although disability and youth researchers have documented and attempted to challenge young disabled people's oppression ('the *effects* of binary opposition'), they have not challenged 'the limit of what is possible and necessary' (Shildrick 2009: 3). Of course, neither can this book complete such a task; to claim completion would in itself be limiting. Nevertheless, I argue that too often approaches to research with young disabled people buy into a reasonable rhetoric of adulthood normativity. This has resulted in a liberal acceptance of *some* disabled people, at the expense of others. This book aims to go beyond normative youth-adult pathways, to question a reasonableness inherent to adulthood discourse. This book should not, however, be thought of as a textbook offering answers. Rather, think of this book as a provocation, a thinking-through, from a particular time and place, which aims to question dyads of un/reasonableness as they function around 'youth', 'disability', 'adult', 'able'.

A Utopian Project of 'Imagining Otherwise'

By chance, in summer 2012 I attended a presentation by Keri Facer (2011a) which introduced me to the academic discipline of 'futurology'. Futurology has its origins in war strategy and continues to be used in the financial sector; concepts that sit uncomfortably with the politics of this book. However, the presentation was about futurology's use within education. At the time I had not yet started my fieldwork and was feeling somewhat conflicted. I was both increasingly annoyed by the conceptualisation of young people as incomplete-adults (Slater 2013a); but also struggling with the paradoxical situation this sometimes left me in. The normative and ableist focus on adulthood futures meant conversations of the future were routinely denied to young disabled people (Haraldsdóttir 2013; Kafer 2013; Slater 2013a). I therefore felt both resistant to focusing on young people's 'adulthood futures' (with the fear of denying the here-and-now experiences of 'being young', and restricting the multiplicities of possibilities there is to become), but also aware that perhaps for these young people, being asked the questions I felt constricted by (have you got a boyfriend? What will you do when you grow up?), were far from 'the norm'.

Facer's (2011a) paper, however, offered me a 'Eureka' moment. She explained that educational (and, as I later discovered, feminist) futurologists argue that the future has been colonised, by Hollywood, corporations and big business. Those outside of these money-making institutions are only encouraged to perform future thinking in terms of how they will individually fit into already established systems (Gunnarsson-Östling 2011; Milojević 2008). Rather than dismissing talk of the future per se, educational futurologists advocate for a shift from talking to young people only about individual futures, to instead encouraging young people to think about societal and collective futures; how the future could function otherwise[3] (Facer 2011b, 2013; Hicks 2002). As people low down the list of those asked about large-scale possibility and change, asking young disabled people for their decolonising and enabling future ideas seemed an important pivoting point.

Exploring how I could utilise futurology in my research led me to utopian texts. Although there are links between futurist thinking and utopias, the two terms are not interchangeable: whereas utopian thinking is about 'the ideal', futurology considers possible, probable and preferable futures (Hicks 2002). I was less interested in what was possible, or probable in my fieldwork, but keen to find out participants' preferable futures. Although drawing on futurist thinking, therefore, I cast my research as utopian, rather than futurist. For More (1972), utopia paradoxically means a 'good place' that is 'no place'. For my purposes, a utopia is a dream or a vision of an ideal world; it does not exist (it is 'no place'), yet it is a place we can strive towards (a 'good place'). 'Utopia is the expression of the desire for a better way of being or of living' (Levitas 2005: 5). Asking young disabled people for their utopian ideas had dual purpose. Firstly, asking for alternative future visions calls for social and political action. Importantly, however, we cannot envisage a 'better place' without simultaneously critiquing the present (Geoghegan 1987; Gordon and Hollinger 2002; Little 2006; Sargisson 2000). Employing 'utopia as method' meant starting by talking to young disabled people about what was wrong with the world around them. This offered participants the agency I was looking for; they could talk to me about themselves, envisaging themselves in the future, or focus on reimagining the world around them.

---

3   Since the time of fieldwork and writing this book, Kafer's (2013) explorations of time and futurity in relation to disability and crip/queer possibility have strongly resonated with my thinking. However, this sadly came too late to occupy a prominent position with the text.

From Reason to Fantasy: The Best Ever Future Worlds Project

> [A] utopian impulse or mentality [... is] grounded in the human capacity, and need, for fantasy; the perpetual conscious and unconscious rearranging of reality and one's place in it. It is the attempt to create an environment in which one is truly at ease. (Geoghegan 1987: 2)

Standing by Geoghegan's (1987) sentiment, young people's fantasies, emotions and desires became intrinsic to my research. If reality is silence (Fuller and Loogma 2009) and truth is dangerous (Gergen 2008), I required a method/ology that put fantasy on loud speaker. As well as giving feminists and educationalists the ground on which to trouble the 'violence of now' through critiquing current patriarchy, futurology and utopian thinking offered me performative potential; space to think about the way things could be. Like youth subcultural researchers whose work I engage with in Chapter 4, methods inspired by utopian thinking, alongside educational and feminist futurology help recast disabled young people's ideas, actions and emotions as political.

What emerged was the The Best-Ever Future Worlds Project, a utopian time-travelling project carried out with young disabled people. My plan: to ask young disabled people to travel forward in time to a world set up just the way they want it. There were three contexts to this:

1. A 10-week art project (10 x two-hour sessions) for seven young people involved in Boom,[4] a charity running visual arts workshops for people with the label of intellectual impairment.

2. Three workshops with 20 young people (with physical, sensory and intellectual impairments) involved in a disabled people's organisation's Youth Forum (YF). This resulted in additional ethnography (and two one-hour recorded interviews) outside of YF with one member, Colin.

3. A three-month ethnography with young disabled activists running an Independent Living Centre (ILC) in Reykjavik, Iceland (NPA Miðstöðin 2013).

I ran the first two strands of The Best Ever Future Worlds Project, with Boom and YF, in the north of England between October 2011 and February 2012. Different methods were employed with different groups of young people. In the UK I planned activities and workshops (facilitated by myself with

---

4   The names of organisations in the UK have been changed for anonymity reasons. As much of what the Independent Living Centre in Iceland do is already in the public sphere, this name has not been changed (on agreement of its board members).

assistance from artists and youth workers) which resulted in the creation of various ideas books, art pieces and posters, as well as (transcribed) interviews and videos. I also relied upon a research diary for both generating and analysing data (Richardson 1998). From The Best-Ever Future Worlds Project with YF grew an additional ethnographic research relationship as I spent time with a young disabled activist, Colin. I also interviewed Coin outside of YF. As with many of the activities and conversations that you'll see integrated into the following chapters, although our interviews began by 'talking utopias', they developed into broader conversations about youth, disability and beyond. In Iceland I chose not to employ the kinds of creative methods used in the UK. Sargisson (2000) argues that those involved in political movements are already engaged in utopian thinking. Therefore, I was interested in how the young people involved in the Independent Living Movement (ILM) in Iceland thought the world could function otherwise. As well as my research diary, data in Iceland included a co-written paper with two Icelandic participants, which was later co-presented at *Manchester Metropolitan University's Child, Youth, Family and Disability Conference* (Slater, Ágústsdóttir and Haraldsdóttir 2012). I will outline specific activities used with young people more fully as and when I use the 'data' collected from them. Similarly, I introduce the young people[5] whose stories I tell more fully as and when their stories are told.

Queer(y)ing

Queer theory allows for a questioning of normativity which makes space for the kinds of 'otherwise' discourses this book aims to uncover (Shildrick 2009). The ideas I present are therefore influenced by queer theory. I use queer as a verb: to queer, to make others think differently, to disrupt the status-quo. Gibson-Graham (1999) uses the term queer(y)ing to describe questioning to seek out possibility and change. Queer(y)ing is an integral part of imagining otherwise with disabled young people, not only when directly considering issues around sexuality – such as in Chapter 5 – but also in order to 'mobilize a productive positivity' (Shildrick 2009: 149). I turn now to consider how a queer(y)ing positionality sits with my writing style.

Halberstam (1998: 13) refers to a queer methodology as a scavenger methodology, 'that uses different methods to produce information on subjects

---

5 All participant names are pseudonyms, aside from Embla and Freyja from the Independent Living Centre in Iceland, who chose to have their real names used in the context of my research. Pseudonyms used for young people in Boom were chosen by the young people, and adopted as their 'time travelling' names. Hence you will hear the stories of people such as Meow, US1234 and Treeman used in later chapters.

who have been deliberately or accidentally excluded'. Although not excluded from research per se, disabled young people are rarely included in the more 'liberating' academic paradigms, such as the new sociology of childhood and youth subcultural studies, and CDS engagement with youth is similarly rare (Curran and Runswick-Cole 2013; Slater 2013b; Wickenden 2010). Disabled young people come low down the list of people asked about large-scale possibility and change.

Like Hughes et al. (2012: 316) I therefore treat 'theory as a resource'; theories developed as political tools should be deployed as and when necessary. Theories in this book are therefore called upon as and when they are helpful. The status given to certain theories over others concerns me; 'academic elitism' meaning the views of some are valued over others, leaving some side-lined by research processes (Barnes 2002). I therefore conceptualise theory as no more or less than trying to make some 'sense out of what [is] happening' (hooks 1994: 61) in order to navigate the world. I also begin with the conviction that we all do theory, and value the theorisations of Foucault and Butler (whose work I will introduce in later chapters) no more than those of my young disabled participants. If a theory sparks off an idea of my own, I utilise it. To justify this, through my writing I map how this idea came about. If an idea comes to me through the words or actions of friends, family or research participants my approach is much the same. As a result, this book employs an essay-based style of writing, where specific theories are introduced at the time of utilisation. This allows the reader to approach chapters individually, or the book as a coherent whole. I signpost later to where particular disciplines and theories are introduced in the book.

Queer(y)ing Ethnography

For us, inquiry is a passionate, embodied, and emotional process as well as an intellectual issue, carried on in the heat (or cool) of our action. (Roets and Goedgeluck 2007: 104)

Yes! This is what it feels like to me! My research has taken me places I never imagined, introduced me to fantastic people, let me think things I never thought I'd think, given me space I never thought I'd have, let me be someone I didn't know I could be. Research isn't just about me – expert, naive, whatever – researcher learning about disability and youth. Perhaps it's egotistical, but for me research has been about me and my relationships with the world around me. My relationships to youth and disability. (Research diary, 27th February 2012, after spending time with young disabled activists in Iceland, reading the above paper and drinking hot chocolate in my favourite Reykjavik cafe)

With its roots in cultural anthropology, ethnography is about a researcher immersing themselves in a culture to try capture and represent their day-to-day experiences (Atkinson and Hammersley 1994). I have certainly felt immersed in the worlds of youth and disability: both theoretically, through reading and writing, and in an embodied sense, by spending time and building relationships with young disabled people; and the two undoubtedly overlap. Two of my participants in particular, Embla and Freyja from Iceland (introduced further in Section 2 of the book), became close friends. I therefore cannot wholly separate the stories of research participants from my own. In Chapters 3–6 you will see my stories are intertwined with those of my participants (Denzin 1998). As Spry (2001: 727) writes: 'human experience is chaotic and messy, requiring a pluralism of discursive and interpretive methods that critically turn texts back upon themselves in the constant emancipation of meaning'. In agreement, I situate my work as an auto/ethnographic project, immersed in CDS and sitting at the intersection of youth and disability. Spry (2001: 710) defines autoethnography as 'a self-narrative that critiques the situatedness of self with others in social contexts'. CDS, auto/ethnography and queer theory all share a commitment to uncertainty, fluidity and becoming subjects (Adams and Holman Jones 2011). I believe research is relational (Roets and Goedgeluck 2007; Tregaskis 2004; Tregaskis and Goodley 2005). A queer(y)ing auto/ethnographic approach blurs the boundaries between self and Other (Holman Jones and Adams 2010; Spry 2001). Advocates argue that one of the strengths of autoethnography is its tendency to make audiences consider their place within writing (Adams and Holman Jones 2011; Spry 2001); inviting them 'to engage in the author's subject matter' (Denzin 1998: 321). My queer(y)ing methodology includes the stories of audiences, both imagined (you have already met Mr Reasonable, and in Chapter 1 you witness my imagined conversation with an imagined government minister) and lived (the interpretations and stories that will resonate with those who read it). I use my own stories, alongside stories of others, to consider the goings-on at the intersection of youth and disability. I choose the term auto/ ethnography with a forward slash, over autoethnography to highlight that the aim of the book is not to tell my story, but to stress that my story is significant and tangled amongst the stories of others (Ellis 2007).

I concur with Roets and Geodgeluck (2007: 104) that research is a 'passionate, embodied and emotional process', and one that I am undoubtedly a part of. Both feminist and CDS scholars have argued that 'scientific' approaches to research (including ethnography), claiming to be objective, have silenced and added to the oppression of marginalised groups. In denying researcher subjectivity, researchers privilege the viewpoint of those already in power (Barnes and Mercer 1997; Haraway 1988; Morris 1992; Oakley 1981). In feminist ethnographic research, researchers are encouraged to keep a research diary in which they record and critically reflect upon their place within the setting, and their biases, thoughts and feelings about the research process (Schwandt 1997; Watt 2007). This adds to and is analysed alongside the researcher's data (Kleinsasser 2000). The process of qualitative inquiry is emergent (Denzin and Lincoln 1994): the researcher is taken on a journey, unsure at the beginning where she will end up at the end. Much of my data relied on my own interpretations of stories through the use of my research diary. Self-reflection must be an iterative and on-going process.

Queer(y)ing Writing

I draw on feminist notions of researcher reflexivity (Guillemin and Gillam 2004) and my voice is overt throughout. Like Watt (2007) my approach to writing has never been a conscious decision resulting from immersion in qualitative theory, but a way to organise my thoughts and not lose track of ideas. I write lots, fairly rapidly, and relate to Richardson (1998: 346) when she says, 'I write because I want to find something out. I write in order to learn something that I didn't know before I wrote it. I was taught, however, as perhaps you were, too, not to write until I knew what I wanted to say, until my points were organized and outlined'. The way I work is probably similar to many researchers. I read stuff and think about stuff. During this time, stuff happens in my life. I hear stories of stuff happening in the lives of my friends. I chat about stuff to people. All of this stuff affects the other stuff, both in terms of the stuff I then choose to do, and the way I think about and conceptualise stuff. I then, and perhaps this is where my writing differs from some more traditionally academic texts, write about this myriad of stuff reflexively, in relation to youth and disability. As a result, this book is littered with stories of myself, my friends and my family, moving in, out and through the phenomena of 'youth' and 'disability'. I think of this as a process of 'writing-to-sort-my-head-out', or as Kleinsasser (2000) perhaps more coherently puts it: writing to unlearn.

Over the course of this book I interweave my own stories and the stories of my participants with a medley of transdisciplinary critical theories demanded by my intersectional approach to research. It is important, therefore, that I queer(y) not just my approach to research; not just the world around me; not just 'youth' and 'disability'; but also myself.

Queer(y)ing Myself

The autoethnographic means telling a story about how much we – children and parents, researchers and subjects, authors and readers – worry about fitting in, about normal, about being accepted, loved, and valued. The queer means telling a story about being half in and half out of identities, subject positions, and discourses and having the courage to be fluid in a world relentlessly searching for stability and certainty. The reflexive means understanding the way stories change and can change. (Holman, Jones and Adams 2010: 114)

At the same time as I started my doctoral studies, many of my friends, along with tens of thousands of other young people were struggling to find work. My Mum and Dad were in the company of many others – stressed, overworked and bullied through macho-competitive managerial systems in a shrinking UK public sector, eventually leading to unemployment. At the same time disabled people such as my uncle were fighting to receive support and benefits crucial to their quality of life/ survival, whilst being scapegoated as burdensome drains on society (Garthwaite 2011). As outlined further over Chapters 1 and 2, for many, the UK is not an easy place to live. Growing up with my lovely Marxist father I was constantly reminded that 'philosophers have interpreted the world, Jen, but the point is to change it', and it is a sentiment that has stuck. Although this resonates with the political motivations of disability studies (Goodley 2011), it has nevertheless made me feel at times uneasy about my life in academia (Slater f.c.).

Part way through doing this research I told some friends, my Mum and my brother, that I was having a relationship with a woman. From my teenage years onwards, I felt hemmed in by questions around my continued un-coupled status: 'have you got a boyfriend?', 'have you got a boyfriend yet?', '*when* will you get a boyfriend?', 'will you *ever* get a boyfriend??' My discomfort with these questions was not so much because of the heterosexual expectation, or a particular desire to be with a girl, but more with, as participants in Goltz's (2009: 574) study put it, the 'you complete me syndrome': I felt I 'should', like my brothers, be coupled with *somebody*.

When I was 15 my best mate 'came out' to me in a German class. 'Jen, I need to tell you something', Paul whispered, as we watched the hyenas march in front of us in *Der Koenig der Loewen*. 'What?' I replied, 'I'm gay'. I wasn't particularly shocked and don't remember my response, but I do remember him 'coming out' to the chemistry class a few weeks later. It was just before his 16th birthday: 'Sixteen Paul, you know what that means?' a lad in the class jibed, 'you'll be legal! That's unless you're ...', 'yeah, it's different if you're gay',[6] Paul bravely replied. I remember proudly recounting the story to Mum: 'I don't see why people have to "come out" like that, it shouldn't have to be such a big deal',

---

6 'Sex between men was illegal until 1967, when the Sexual Offences Act came into force in England and Wales and made it legal for two men aged 21 and over to have sex. In 1994 the age that gay men could legally have sex was lowered to 18, and in 2001 it was finally lowered to 16 – making it equal to the age of consent for straight people' (Stonewall 2010).

Mum replied. It was a big deal though. Another friend, openly gay before Paul's declaration, was beaten up at the school gates on numerous occasions.

Four years later, as an undergraduate disability studies student, I was introduced to queer theory. I tried to convince my Mum how cool it was. 'It's like, why do we put people in these boxes? Why do you have to be gay or straight? That's what queer theory's about. I've never thought about it before. You shouldn't have to declare yourself one thing or the other'. Mum's reply surprised me: 'I don't know, Jen, it just seems like common sense to me'. I remember being a bit disappointed by her reaction. At the age of 23, immersed in various critical theories troubling normativity, and blessed with a brilliant family that had taught me the importance of putting-the-world-to-rights, I wasn't worried to tell Mum of my new same-gender relationship. Yet, neither was I surprised when she responded, 'How long have you known you were gay, then?' I explained to her that 'coming out gay' was not what I was doing – this is not what it felt like. I just wanted to share with her a relationship that I was excited about. 'It's not about her being a girl', I said. Mum smiled, 'Ohhhh, I knew you'd say that!'

Mum then reassured me, 'your Dad doesn't care what anybody does'. Knowing my Dad, I know he, like my Mum, doesn't care what 'anybody does', in terms of sexuality anyway. If I declared I voted Tory, joined the British National Party or enlisted in the army, he and my Mum would care what I did. I later laughed about Mum's reassurance with my brother: why should Dad care 'what anybody does'? Mum's statement, however, appears *reasonable*, because people do care 'what people do'. People continue to suffer for 'what they want to do'. These two statements signal that even in my wonderful, nothing-but-supportive family, there are norms around what people are expected to do and be. By asking when I 'knew' I was gay, and assuring me 'Dad doesn't care what anybody does', the heterosexual expectation emerges through their stalwart attempts to not impose anything.

Exploring stories such as this is one aim of this book. What expectations do we put on young people growing-up? How do these vary when we consider infinite intersecting factors shaping lives? I share this story because it highlights how my immersion in theory (queer, disability, feminist, and so on) has given me the time and space to consider youth and disability and my place within it. I wonder if without them I would have been able to resist the heterosexual expectation: would I have been able to, wanted to, or considered queer as a possibility? Secondly, it highlights the hybridity of identity. When I was 15 and Paul told me he was gay, I never considered that just a few years later my mate would be an international drag queen. Neither did I consider the fluidity of sexuality; that maybe I was 'not-straight' either. I do know, however, that my experiences of coming out 'not-straight' with the words CDS has given me and the circles it has allowed me access to, were decidedly easier (not a big deal), than for my friends in a big Yorkshire comprehensive school (definitely a big deal). Through my studies, I have been able to, and have *enjoyed* the process of queer(y)ing myself and the world around me. I have been given the opportunity to grow into a queer(y)ing space.

I am not disabled, perhaps I am or perhaps I am not on the fringes of youth. I'm maybe not-straight-but-not-gay-either – something I've come to learn as queer. If I'm honest, I can 'pass' as any one of the privileged positions these identities entail. However, these fluid and between positionalities, along with my other intersecting identities of white, former-PhD student/now academic, woman, from Wakefield, Yorkshire, England affect how I do research. Researching at the intersection of 'youth' and 'disability' has been an iterative process: it has had a profound impact on me, which has impacted on how I do my research, which has impacted on me, and so on. Critics have deemed autoethnography a self-indulgent process (Sparkes 2002), a critique that has not passed me by. However, whether or not it is self-indulgent, to not write myself into this book would seem not only 'bad research', but unethical (Kleinsasser 2000).

Queer(y)ing Ethics

The auto/ethnographical stance I take brings with it ethical concerns. In sharing my stories, I am also sharing the stories of others (Ellis and Bochner 2000). I have told you about my friends who cannot find work; my Mum and Dad, uncle and brothers; Paul, the jibing boy in the chemistry class, and the female–female relationship. Chapters 3–6 will share the stories of my disabled participants – who were also my peers and some of whom became my friends. Adams and Holman Jones (2011: 109) ask, 'what of the stories we want to tell because they are so important and enraging and courageous and hopeful but don't because they are not ours – alone – to tell?' I have sought the consent of my participants, yet the partial and connected nature of stories (Ellis 2007) means that in telling any story, I am going to tread on the stories of others. Without denying the above, the ethical dilemmas I have struggled with through my queer(y)ing auto/ethnographical approach, have also had ethical benefits. Firstly, these ethical concerns forced me to take ethics beyond university procedural concerns[7] (considering, for example, the implications of forming friendships through research). Moreover, however, I follow Etherington (2007) and Guillemin and Gillam (2004) in seeing the sharing of stories as an ethical practice.

Worrying about ethics alone and with others was a constant force in my research: whether it be the ethics of being in paid employment when people around me are struggling to survive; the ethics of writing about, and therefore

---

7   The research proposal was passed through a university ethics committee, who deemed it ethically sound. Also see previous footnotes on pseudonyms.

reifying an already scrutinising gaze on disabled young people (Priestley 2003); or the ethics of blurring the boundaries between friendships and research (Brooks 2006; Ellis 2007; Tillmann-Healy 2003). These worries emerge from Chapter 3 onwards. Perhaps Josselson is correct, however, when she writes:

> I would worry most if I stopped worrying, stopped suffering for the disjunction that occurs when we try to tell the Other's story. To be uncomfortable with this work, I think, protects us from going too far. It is with our anxiety, dread, guilt, and shame that we honor our participants. To do this work we must contain these feelings rather than deny, suppress, or rationalize them. We must at least try to be fully aware of what we are doing. (Josselson 1996: 70)

Mapping this Book

Through the chapters that follow my discussions revolve around the following question: what would it mean to remove the adulthood full-stop from youth, and instead think of it as part of the continual becoming of life? And what can 'disability' teach us in this quest? To explore this question, my engagement with Mr Reasonable allows us to move beyond a liberal and unquestioning rhetoric of 'sameness', to instead critically theorise 'difference', largely as it functions through developmental discourse, under the ableist, white supremacist, and heteropatriarchal structures of global capitalism. I begin making the case for such a positioning in Chapter 1; unpicking the 'liberal' from the 'neoliberal', I argue a liberal narrative of disabled people as 'just the same as everybody else' fails to challenge normativity. Whilst busily arguing 'sameness' we don't stop to ask who this 'everybody else' is. Thus, we continue to fight for the rights of those already in power (our Mr Reasonable, if you will). A sometimes well-intentioned liberal discourse can therefore work to support the conditions of neoliberalism. I thus choose to follow Sothern (2007) in complicating the liberal/neoliberal distinction, employing the term (neo)liberalism in the remainder of the book.

I further investigate the 'everyone else' of (neo)liberal adulthood over Chapter 2. Here I draw on Lesko (2012) to view youth, not as an implicit stage of child-adult development, but as a policed and ideological border zone. Unpicking the workings at the border zone of youth, we see not just the ableist, but the racist and patriarchal roots of development theory. The requirements of the 'everyone else' of adulthood therefore become clearer: to be accepted as adult, one must adopt the laws of whiteness, comply with gender binaries and prove oneself 'able'. Under (neo)liberalism to be 'able' also means being the self-sustaining, productive citizen who is not poor. We see the need for intersectional interrogation of ableism at the border zone of youth.

Despite the injustice of adulthood becoming more recognisable, I explore in Chapter 3 how adulthood normativity works around a discourse of 'reason' and 'reasonableness', to normalise this marginalisation and oppression. Introducing the first of stories from young disabled people that took part in my research, I explore how 'reason' functions in the lives of young people with whom I spent time. Considering reason along axes of disability, as it intertwines with youth, gender, race, bodies and sexuality, I argue that to be considered 'reasonable' is sometimes a matter of survival. However, this tactic of survival is never without its consequences. In the stories I share there is no rest from a becoming-adult endeavour. Moreover, asserting one's sameness in order to be understood as 'reasonable' often means further distancing oneself from other forms of Otherness, and therefore complying with systemic forms of marginalisation. What we lose through rhetoric of becoming-reasonable-adult is the space to 'become' in any multitude of ways. Chapter 3 also illuminates for us the relationship between 'reason' and 'autonomy'; leading us into Chapter 4.

In Chapter 4, I engage with some contested debates in critical disability studies: whether to reject or refashion notions of 'the individual' and with this 'independence'. I frame this chapter through the relationships between young people and their parents in order to explore the implications of an expected shift from childhood dependence to adulthood independence. Unlike poststructuralist thinkers who have rejected notions of the individual (e.g. B.E. Gibson 2006; B.E. Gibson, Brooks, DeMatteo and King 2009; B.E. Gibson, Carnevale and King 2012; Shildrick 2009), I follow Greenstein and Graby (2013) by taking lessons from disabled people's critiques of 'independence', and feminist debates of 'autonomy'. I argue through this chapter that youth is not about becoming-independent-adult, but part of the continual becoming-of-life. Furthermore, this becoming is a continually struggle (together) for relational autonomy which is always dependent upon structures of power.

Chapter 5 continues the discussion of relationships by critically engaging with young disabled people's negotiations of space at the border zone of youth. Here I come to youth subcultural studies, a discipline that has been given the rare accolade of offering positive here-and-now stories of 'being young' (Hodkinson 2008). Yet, I find this to be a discipline that has rarely engaged with disability or disability studies (Fitzgerald and Kirk 2009). Nevertheless, I find some classic youth subcultural texts (Corrigan 2006; McRobbie 1980, 2000; McRobbie and Garber 2000; Willis 1977) useful in complicating notions of 'access' (Titchkosky 2011) as it relates to youth culture. I explore the embodied ways in which young disabled people are both doing and asserting themselves as 'youth'. If, as McRobbie (2000: 45) tells us 'the "cultural" is always a site for struggle and conflict', I wonder why the experiences of the young disabled people I spent time with, weren't considered (normatively) 'youth cultural'.

Chapter 6 also engages with notions of 'what it is to be young'. Here I draw on Mingus' essay, *Moving Toward the Ugly: A Politic Beyond Desirability* to have 'difficult conversations' at the intersections of gender, sexuality, disability and the youthful body. This chapter brings together some of the themes considered throughout the book, to show the importance of including disability as part of wider intersectional conversations. Ableism is marked as inherently intersectional, as I argue that the conceptualisation of certain bodies as *unreasonable* is part of larger structures of violence.

Finally in the closing chapter I bring together some of what we've learnt through this book, as we wave goodbye to Mr Reasonable.

Chapter 1
Disabled People in
(Neo)liberal Times
(or, Disability as Unreasonable)

The aim of this book isn't particularly one of policy interrogation. This is not to say, however, that social, political and cultural contexts are not important. As outlined in the Introduction, setting 'disability' in social, political and cultural contexts is one of the overarching aims of a disability studies project (Goodley 2011). This book was mainly written in the north of England between September 2010 and August 2014, with three months spent doing fieldwork in Iceland between February and May 2012. In May 2010, four months before my youth and disability project began, and amidst the 'global financial crisis', a Conservative/Liberal Democrat coalition government ended the 12-year reign of New Labour in the UK.[1] Following the work of previous Conservative Prime Ministers Margaret Thatcher and John Major, between 1998 and 2010 New Labour enforced a series of backhanded privatisations (Roulstone and Prideaux 2011). Schools were re-branded as academies and affiliated with big businesses, whilst agendas such as *Every Child Matters* conceptualised the child as entrepreneurial (Goodley and Runswick-Cole 2011a). However, since the arrival of the coalition government neoliberal mantras of 'individuality, personal fulfilment and entrepreneurial responsibility' (Sothern 2007: 147) have become louder and stronger. At the time of writing, Britain's public services are being eroded as local councils make significant cutbacks. This, of course, has political consequences which impact upon young and disabled people. It also impacts upon the way in which researchers go about researching 'youth' and 'disability'. The aim of this chapter is to begin unpicking both previous research around 'youth' and 'disability' as well as the context in which the young disabled people I spent time with were living (an unpicking that will continue into Chapter 2).

---

1 Although some of my fieldwork took place in Iceland, this chapter and the next chapter take the UK as the political context. However, this should be taken as an example of (neo)liberal policy which can be used to frame the latter chapters, rather than a context to which the arguments made are unique. As Peck and Tickell (2002: 380) write 'neoliberalism seems to be everywhere'.

I contextualise this book in what are recurrently deemed 'neoliberal times', and begin this chapter by further exploring the term 'neoliberalism'. To do this, I consider the relationship between 'liberalism' and 'neoliberalism' further. I agree with Sothern (2007) that this relationship is one which is often neglected and I therefore start with a discussion of 'liberalism'. I find that much disability studies research around youth makes an argument of 'liberal acceptance': that disabled young people are 'just the same as everybody else'. Yet, as I go on to think more about the neoliberal context, I worry that an argument of 'sameness' can play into the hands of politicians who are trying to justify public-service cuts through neoliberal rhetoric. Therefore, this chapter argues that we need to be wary of liberal arguments which aim to counter neoliberal doctrine, as they often fail to include those most precariously positioned. I thus explain why I will follow Sothern (2007) in complicating the distinction between the 'liberal' and the 'neoliberal' by employing the phrase (neo)liberalism.

Liberalism, Disabled Young People, and the Rhetoric of 'Sameness'

Last week I shared with my friend Hari a discussion I'd had with my family around queer relationships. The conversation in question was similar to the story I shared in the introductory chapter: there was an insistence that, so long as they're not hurting anybody, other people's relationships (whatever they may look like) shouldn't be anything to do with anyone except those involved – we should just let people get on with it. Hari's response was that I was lucky to have such a 'liberal' family. In some ways Hari was correct, I am lucky, as my discussion in the introductory chapter identified, my family made it very easy for me to talk to them about my own queer relationships. Yet, my family's relationship with 'liberalism' is one I'd contest; what it means to be 'liberal' needs some further investigation.

Scott and Marshall (2009: 415) identify liberalism as being about 'the free exercise of religion, speech, and association'. In my conversation with Hari, he was identifying the 'liberal' argument of personal freedom that my family were using. The 'empowerment', 'equality' and 'freedom' we may associate with liberalism are largely accepted as a 'good thing' within capitalist democracies (Sothern 2007). As a politically-left, queer woman it would perhaps be assumed I would agree with the argument that people's relationships (whatever they may look like) are 'their own business'. And, to an extent, I do. Yet, the situation is more complicated than this liberal statement allows. The public/private divide is loaded with power dynamics, not all of which have positive implications for marginalised groups (Sherry 2004). As I discussed in the introductory chapter, the liberal argument that we should all just be able to 'get on with stuff' doesn't problematise (in this case) the pervasiveness of heteronormativity (the expectation of heterosexuality, which is projected as the ideal), or the differing degrees of privilege other intersecting identities create. This means a) those who don't identify as heterosexual are positioned as Other; and b) those deemed outside 'liberally accepted' homosexuality remain peripheral (Warner 2003, also discussed in Chapter 6 of this book).

The above is a deliberate simplification used to exemplify the common-sense usage of the word 'liberal'. If we continue to interrogate 'liberalism' from its roots we can see more contradictions emerging. The eighteenth century, known as the *Age of Enlightenment*, saw the American and French revolutions, where French people overthrew the monarchy and American people declared independence from British colonial rule (which was also functioning under a monarchy). This meant a change, from a sovereign rule by divine right, to the creation of a 'representative democracy'. For Americans, two (continually prevailing) mantras of liberal democracy came out of this. Firstly, Thomas Jefferson's (1776) statement in the *American Declaration of Independence* that 'all men are created equal'; and secondly, a system based on the law of 'one man, one vote'. You may have already noted here the gendered pronouns used to found liberal democracy: 'All *men* are created equal'; 'one *man*, one vote'. Furthermore, there was another overt contradiction within this ideology. Gender aside, although all men were supposedly created equal, this was also the time of the slave trade. The valid subject of liberal freedom and democracy, therefore, was not only male, but also white.

Why I am giving this history lesson? Surely things are different now? We are living in the post-civil rights era. There have been feminist movements. *Our* Western civilisations are based upon democracies where men and women have the vote, despite colour. Liberalism has moved on from its origins and is now about personal freedom and equality to which we are *all* (man and woman; white and black), entitled to: right?! Elements of this are true. Social movements, such as civil rights movements, feminist movements, lesbian, gay, bisexual, trans*[2] (LGBT*), queer movements and disabled people's movements have argued that those considered Other (people of colour, women, queer and intersex people, and disabled people) should be embedded and given equal rights within this liberal democracy (Davis 2002; Erevelles 1996; Sedgwick 1990). This has been done by arguing these subjugated positions into a rhetoric of 'sameness', ultimately boiling down to the argument that fundamentally, *biologically*, we are the same as you, and should therefore enjoy the same freedoms (Erevelles 1996). Liberal feminists, for example, have argued that women's biology should be no less valued than that of men; anti-racist scholars and activists have argued that

---

2   I include the asterisk (*) in the word 'trans' to indicate that I am not only referring to those who identify as trans men or trans women, but also those who do not identify as 'men' or 'women' (people that identify, for example, as non-binary, genderqueer or genderless).

there is no correlation between 'race' and 'ability' (Erevelles 1996); and, recently, queer activists have argued that LGBT* people should have the same right to marriage as heterosexual people (Sullivan 2004). Perhaps most pertinently for our 'youth' and 'disability' discussions, disabled people, through an argument of equality (Crow 2012), 'have demanded the right to be regarded as valued participants within mainstream society' (Erevelles 1996: 519).

Erevelles (1996), however, has concerns about the sustainability of an argument of 'sameness' for disabled people. She highlights that when not coming in direct relation to disability, arguments of 'sameness' often function at the *expense* of disabled people. Historically, for example, people of colour were viewed as less 'intelligent' than white people. In order to counter their positioning as subordinate, anti-racist activists have (rightly) denied any correlation between 'race' and 'intelligence' by arguing that there is no biological difference between themselves and white people. Yet, through doing so, rather than recognising the shared historical oppressions between people of colour and disabled people (further investigated in Chapter 2), some anti-racism activists separate themselves from disabled people. Furthermore, Erevelles (1996) points out that an argument around a lack of 'biological difference' is harder to maintain for disabled people than those fighting for and from other identity positionings. Denying biological difference through an argument of sameness means that if barriers to sameness are removed, and some disabled people continue to fail, blame can be placed upon individuals meaning their 'exclusion from culture is more justified than ever' (Ferguson and Ferguson 2001: 84).

This critique becomes pertinent when we consider the in/exclusivity of disabled people's movements. It has been argued that disabled people with labels of 'intellectual impairment' have been left aside by both disabled people's movements and disability studies (Boxall, Carson and Docherty 2004; Goodley 2001; Walmsley 2001). This is not an argument unique to conversations of disability. Similar arguments have been made by activists and scholars working from other identity positionings. Black feminists such as Crenshaw (1989), hooks (1994) and Lorde (2012), for example, point out that liberal feminist movements work on ideals of 'whiteness', and a theorising of gender which is not intersectional and which therefore excludes the combination of racism and sexism experienced by black women. Queer scholars and activists have noted that the focus on marriage equality in liberally based LGBT* and queer movements privileges homosexual people willing to fit into heterosexual frameworks at the expense of those unwilling/ unable to comply (McRuer 2006; Warner 2003). Furthermore, often when claiming to address LGBT* issues, the experiences of trans* people are left aside (Collins 2011; Waite 2013). Arguments of liberal acceptance can mean fighting for the rights of the 'dominant, often white, male, "normal" subject' (Davis 2002), at the expense of other ways of being. Rather than challenging dominant ideals, we are all expected to 'fit into' the very ideals that have served to exclude us. Thus, for Sothern (2007: 147) an 'intolerability towards difference' is apparent in both 'liberal' and 'neoliberal' doctrine. In Chapter 2 I will propose that an argument that disabled young people are 'just the same as everybody else' fails to challenge (neo)liberal ideals of the pedestalled adult subject. For now, however, I turn to further explore why it might be both tempting and dangerous to employ a liberal argument of sameness in neoliberal times. I begin by further outlining the term 'neoliberal'.

What is 'Neoliberalism', Anyway?

Peck and Tickell (2002: 380) write that 'neoliberalism seems to be everywhere'. By this, they not only mean that neoliberalism infiltrates all aspects of life – something we will think more about throughout the book – but that it is continually evoked as '*the* explanatory term for contemporary forms of economic restructuring' in academic texts (Larner 2003: 509, original emphasis). Although Peck and Tickell (2002) ground their work in geography, the same statement could be made about disability studies; neoliberalism is repeatedly cited as the grounding political context to be considered. For example, in 2012 the Lancaster Disability Studies Conference (arguably the largest UK-based disability studies conference) chose *Disability, Poverty and Neo-Liberalism* as the conference theme. This is understandable; neoliberalism is usually (for good reason) evoked as a political context which disabled people do not fare well within and it therefore requires interrogation. Yet terms such as 'neoliberalism', 'neo-liberalism', 'global neoliberalism' and 'neoliberal capitalism' are often used seemingly interchangeably, with little explanation. The way we define our terms makes a difference to the argument we are making (terms are played around with and redefined throughout the book). I want to explain through the rest of this chapter why I find it useful to follow Sothern (2007) in evoking the term (neo)liberalism.

Neoliberalism is largely associated with the politics of the right. It involves an economic restructuring through a (rhetorical, at least – considered further below) weakening of the state in favour of big business, competition and the global free-market economy (Peck and Tickell 2002). The turn to neoliberalism is usually attributed to the late 1970s and 1980s, and the rule of Reagan (in the USA) and Thatcher (in Britain). This era saw an upsurge in free-market thinking. In Britain, for example, Thatcher privatised over 50 previously state-owned companies including British Transport Docks, British Telecoms, British Gas, British Steel, as well as water and electricity. Such a neoliberal positioning – complete domination of the free market – is often seen as oppositional to a post-war state of affairs where the welfare state was strong. In fact, whereas it is often assumed that the post-war years were built on 'pulling together' and a sense of community, in a 1987 interview with the magazine, *Woman's Own*, Thatcher famously proclaimed that 'there is no such thing as society' (Keay 1987).

Thatcher's statement sums up a neoliberal politic of personal responsibility. Yet Sothern (2007) argues that positioning neoliberalism as anti-society does not sufficiently capture the pervasiveness, complexities or contradictions of neoliberal doctrines. If we continue our brief history, the merits of Sothern's argument become clearer. Thatcher was followed by another Conservative Prime Minister, John Major, until 1997 when New Labour took power, with Tony Blair as Prime Minister. A New Labour government, however, did not mean a return to the previous era of a strong state. Instead, during the 1990s and into the 2000s, the neoliberal doctrine continued, albeit less overtly (Peck and Tickell 2002; Roulstone and Prideaux 2011; Yates and Roulstone 2012). Rather than complete privatisation, New Labour argued for a 'third way' where the private and public were brought together (Owen and Harris 2012). Privatisation was more 'backhanded': previously state-run schools, for example, were granted 'academy status', freed from local authority control and often sponsored by big businesses. This gave (amongst other things) academies more freedom over the curriculum, the opportunity to employ non-qualified teachers, less obligations in terms of teachers' pay scales and conditions, and more choice over which students they allowed in (ALLFIE's 2012, positionality statement on academies gives a good account of what this means for disabled students). Similarly, parts of the National Health Service (NHS) became subject to a 'creeping privatisation'; services such as catering and cleaning, for example, were tenured out. The overall (neoliberal) message of the Labour government was that work should pay – and it was the responsibility of the individual to be a player in the market (Owen and Harris 2012). For sceptics, however, this meant the removal of life-sustaining supports and services.

We begin to see here some links between 'liberal' arguments of equity and inclusion and 'neoliberal' discourses of personal responsibility. Disabled people have, for good reason, argued that they should have equal access to the economy – and this means, amongst other things, removing barriers to work (Oliver 1990). Attempts have been made to answer (or, to the more sceptical, pacify) these cries through legislation. For example, in the UK, the *Equality Act 2010* means that an 'employer has to make 'reasonable adjustments' to avoid you [disabled people] being put at a disadvantage compared to non-disabled people in the workplace. For example, adjusting your working hours or providing you with a special piece of equipment to help you do the job' (DirectGov 2011). Although on the surface this seems good, we yet again say hello to our friend Mr Reasonable. The demand of access must be a 'reasonable' one. We know from the social model that the problem is one of inaccessible working practices and environments, not one of individual bodies (Oliver 1990). Yet, Mr Reasonable's most able response to the question of access is to individualise: 'you cannot access work due to disability. But, as we are Reasonable Men, we will meet your individual access demands, if they too are Reasonable'. As Titchkosky (2011: 77) tells us, seeking reason for demands of accessibility means that 'whether or not the reasons for lack of access are judged good or bad, the social activity of people seeking reasons fosters the sensibility that lack of access is reasonable'. As a result, the bodies of those for whom work remains inaccessible, are deemed unreasonable; '"naturally" a problem for some spaces' (Titchkosky 2011: 35). Although the parameters may be slightly widened, the changes made through 'neoliberal' rationales, based on 'liberal' arguments of equity, mean that the problem of structures and systems which imagine a narrow range of 'able' bodies and subjects is sustained.

I return to questions of 'access' in Chapter 5. For now, however, I want to continue our journey on the (partially accessible) train of (neo)liberalism. One may imagine that since the Conservative/Liberal Democrat coalition took power in 2010 (led by Conservative Prime Minister David Cameron) the return to neoliberalism would be overt. To an extent this is true, using the 'financial crises' as justification, the coalition has rolled out what they have termed 'welfare reform' in order to cut public spending. With this, the aim to shrink the welfare state – which as Owen and Harris (2012) point out, is a key feature of neoliberal policies – has been made clear. This has, of course, impacted on young and disabled people. In 2012, research done by *Scope* told us that 'disabled people and their carers have seen their income collectively cut by £500m in the past two years' (P. Butler 2012b). In the same year a report from *The Institute for Fiscal Studies* warned that those hardest hit by The Coalition's austerity programme were families with children; those least well-off, losing out most of all (Elliott 2012). Families with disabled children, it has been consistently shown, are proportionally more likely to live in poverty than those without (Every Disabled Child Matters 2007, 2011; Sharma 2002). Recent research highlighted that one-in-seven working families with disabled children and one-in-four without work are missing meals (Every Disabled Child Matters 2012), whilst one-in-six working and one-in-three non-working families with disabled children are left unable to pay to heat their homes (Every Disabled Child Matters 2012). These harsh political times were the backdrop to the research drawn upon in this book.

Although we can draw parallels between retrenchment (the reduction of public spending) now and in the 1980s, the rhetoric through which retrenchment is happening is different. Unlike in 1978 when Thatcher asserted that that there is 'no such thing as society' (Keay 1987), in 2010 David Cameron announced his plans for '*The Big Society*'. Through *The Big Society*, emerging in a dramatically altered political landscape post-Thatcher, Cameron shifted the goal posts. Cameron's argument was that a reduction in spending didn't need to mean a closure of services, but a shift in relations. For example, whereas previously it was the state's responsibility to provide public services such as libraries and youth clubs, now in many places the onus was put onto local communities to step in and run such services. In announcing *The Big Society* Cameron said:

> You can call it liberalism. You can call it empowerment. You can call it freedom. You can call it responsibility. I call it the Big Society. The Big Society is about a huge culture change – where people don't always turn to officials, local authorities or central government for answers to the problems they face but instead feel both free and powerful enough to help themselves and their own communities. (Cameron 2010, 19th July)

Before I go on, it should first be acknowledged that, although since its launch in 2010 talk of *The Big Society* seems to have quietened, the ideology behind 'this huge culture change' remains pertinent and obvious. Libraries throughout the country, for example, are being taken out of state control, instead being put in the hands of community groups, often without the necessary funding, support, or the expertise of a paid, qualified librarian (CILIP 2012). For Runswick-Cole and Goodley (2011: 883) Cameron's vision is not so much one of 'empowerment', but 'attribut[ing] the underlying causes of poverty to the failings of individuals rather than to socio-economic structural factors'. There are words in Cameron's speech that shout of neoliberal politics: a call for 'personal responsibility' and 'helping oneself'. Confusingly, however, Cameron also evokes the word 'liberalism'. Can this be the same 'liberalism' that was evoked when my family discussed same-gender relationships? This is confusing, as my Mum and Dad are in no way advocates of Cameron's ideologies. The similarity in both arguments, however, is that they rely upon both the division of public and private, and a 'freedom to get on with stuff'. The difference is whereas my parents advocate for people to be able to privately 'get on with stuff' in terms of relationships, Cameron wants people to 'get on with stuff' to do with providing previously state-run services. For me, neither liberal argument is satisfactory. Whereas the former doesn't sufficiently critique gender binaries that lead to homophobia (which will be considered further in Chapters 2 and 6), the only 'equality' evoked by the latter is the 'equality of opportunity to become unequal' (Barton 1993: 241).

Runswick-Cole and Goodley (2011) point out that a *Big Society* ideal relies on a subject who is inherently 'able'. However, rather than erase disability from the consciousness of the *Big Society*, disability appears through discourse of charity as *The Big Society* advocates a shift back from rights granted by the state, to a model of philanthropy (Runswick-Cole and Goodley 2011). Given the 'rights not charity' mantra of the disabled people's movement, this is pertinent. I want to consider this further by turning now to look more closely around the positioning of disabled people within (neo)liberal Britain. I do this by not only thinking about structural inequalities, but also discourse and representation that surround 'disability' (and therefore also 'ability').

From the Material to the Discursive (and Back Again): 'Youth' and 'Disability' in (Neo)liberal Britain

As perhaps you have now gathered, Britain under both New Labour and (arguably more so) the coalition government has been a place of contradiction. For example, despite an ever more unstable job market, there has been an increasing emphasis put on the importance of work, as the coalition government aimed to reduce the number of people claiming benefits. Paradoxically, however, this state retrenchment has simultaneously meant disabled people losing the very support that allowed them to work. The Independent Living Fund (ILF), for example, which many disabled people used to hire their own personal assistance which allowed them to work, has been quietly disbanded. A shift from Disability Living Allowance (DLA) to Personal Independence Payments (PIP) meant almost a third of working-age disabled people no longer qualified for the enhanced mobility component of DLA that previously enabled them to lease a vehicle, which in turn allowed many to reach their workplaces (P. Butler 2012a). There have also been cuts to the Access to Work scheme, which allowed disabled people assistance at work. Yet, at the same time, the coalition government are justifying such cuts by representing those who were reliant on state support as 'lazy' and 'scroungers' (Garthwaite 2011).

Drawing on Dyer, Titchkosky (2000) reminds us that representations are not a 'true' reflection of 'reality'. Representations cannot reflect the extensity and complexity of 'reality'. One representation cannot represent a heterogeneous group of people. Representation is dependent on interpretation. A representation cannot be isolated and only works in relation to other representations. Nevertheless, these representations of disabled people as 'scroungers' have had very 'real' consequences. Shockingly illustrating one such consequence, in 2011 a survey reported that since cuts to welfare and benefits, disabled people had suffered not only more poverty and material inequality, but also increased hostility, discrimination and physical attacks as ministers portrayed 'all people with disabilities as scroungers as they seek to cut the number of people on disability benefits' (Boffey 2011: n.p.). Disgracefully, this was happening to the majority of disabled people on at least a weekly basis. 'Unreal' representations around disabled people were impacting on 'real' lives in violent ways. Furthermore, Titchkosky helps us to think about another consequence of representation when she writes:

… consequences [of representations] go beyond the people being represented, since there are consequences for those who make the representations as well. The most authoritative representations of disabled persons arise from medical and/ or therapeutic disciplines, and the social sciences. Anyone who is to be regarded as 'in the know' about disability must show that they know what is the problem and the more details they possess of the problem, the better. This is the 'official textbook' of disability represented in our culture. (Titchkosky 2000: n.p.)

The textbook of disability teaches us that disability is a problem. Left unchallenged, 'official textbook' representations serve to maintain established orders and hierarchies. The aim of disability studies is to challenge 'official textbooks' of disability. As Titchkosky tells us, however, textbooks of disability don't only tell us about 'disability', but also the supposed norm of 'ability'. Representations of disability through the cuts, therefore, also do something else: they mask, create, and reinforce inequality, by inciting a culture of 'us' ('able', 'normal' people) and 'them' (disabled people).

For example, in 2011 the coalition government announced their plans for another policy aiming to reduce public spending: 'The Removal of the Spare Bedroom Subsidy' or, as it more commonly became known 'The Bedroom Tax'. This meant that housing benefit for working-aged people would be linked to property size – those deemed to have more bedrooms than 'necessary' would be penalised through the removal of benefits. *BBC News* (2011) told the story of wheelchair-user Sandra Ruddicks. Since Sandra's family have now grown-up and moved out, we were told that she lived alone in the specially adapted two-bed social housing property in which she brought up her children. Under the reform, we are told that Sandra, along with an estimated 108,000 other disabled people, could be forced to leave their homes, as they are considered to be taking up unnecessary space. At the end of the broadcast, Lord Freud,[3] the Conservative Minister for Welfare Reform, legitimised the move, arguing the importance of people living in houses that are the 'right size for them', in order for it to be fair on the 'ordinary person who does not depend on benefits'. Yet, during the broadcast, nobody asked Lord Freud about his eight bedroom

---

3   As Lord Freud will become a bigger player in this chapter, it seems only fair to fill you in with more details. Former advisor to the Labour Party, Freud drew up plans to revise the welfare system, publishing the 2008 *Welfare to Work* Green Paper which called for measures to get more disabled people and lone parents into work. Although many Labour backbenchers opposed Freud's proposals, it was music to the ears of Tory ministers. In February 2009 Freud controversially joined the Conservative Party as Shadow Minister for Welfare and was given life peerage in the House of Lords. As Minister for Welfare, Freud is the architect of *The Welfare Reform Act 2012*, the implications of which are critiqued in this chapter. He is the grandson of Sigmund Freud.

country mansion which he lives in at the weekend, or his four bedroom townhouse that he inhabits during the week (Mudie 2013). At no point was it suggested that he downsize, to make it fair for the 'ordinary person'.

So what's going on when government ministers speak of the 'ordinary person'? Through such broadcasts, we are delivered a message of self which juxtaposes the disabled person as a deficient and burdensome Other. When 'the ordinary person' is used in this way in current economic times, the story goes as such: We are in a financial mess, that, we know. But, do not worry, ordinary people, for government ministers have found the problem! That problem is the Other: the disabled, the benefit claimant. It is not *us* that are to blame – meaning me, you, the ministers ... the presumption is that you (the watcher/ reader/listener) are one of *us*, not one of *them* (Titchkosky 2000). No, it is not *us* that have created this problem; me and you, *we* are the *ordinary*, the *normal* people – *we* are in this together. It is *them* you should be blaming: the disabled, the benefit claimant, the scroungers. It is *them* that got *us* into this mess (Sloan 2010). But, of course, culture's *'ordinary* man' is law's *'reasonable* man' (Campbell 2009). If, therefore, I was to report to a government minister that I am one of *them* (I *am* the disabled, the benefit claimant – 'I *am* your scrounger'), he would respond (with an awkward chuckle and a pat on the head), that he knows some people are *really* disabled, *really* in need, *really* deserving: 'I'm a reasonable man, Miss Slater' – (at which point I remind him, for the third time, he can call me Dr Slater) – 'but, Miss Slater, there are some people out there taking advantage of us reasonable, ordinary people'.

The above tale is of course not true, but an imagination. I have never met and had the above conversation with a government minister. I would argue though that my imagined, untrue conversation is closer to a 'truth' than the very untrue representation of disabled people as scroungers. Yet we have seen from the increases in violence highlighted by the Scope survey that the depiction of disabled people as a drain on society is an untruth with very 'real' consequences (Boffey 2011). Furthermore, if we critique the above conversation from a disability studies point of view, we are left in a (neo)liberal bind. In the broadcast outlined above, Freud is implying that Sandra, disabled people and other benefit claimants are 'unordinary', 'abnormal' and over-entitled people. We have already seen above that conversations about disability as 'abnormality' have been countered in disability studies through the liberal argument that disabled people are 'just the same as everybody else'. The temptation could be to employ the argument here again: Sandra is not the Other; she, and other disabled people, are no different from anybody else. Yet, such an argument could be dangerous. Once an 'ordinary person', 'the same' as 'anybody else', you have gained the 'equality of opportunity to become unequal' (Barton 1993: 241); any inequality experienced is therefore deemed only to be a result of personal failure and deficit to exploit that opportunity. Although disabled people have insisted that they require support to achieve equality, this particular part of the message, it seems, isn't so easily taken up by the advocates of (neo)liberal politics.

I am reminded through our imagined conversation of Foucault's (1973) notion of gaze. The nineteenth century, Foucault (1977) argued, saw a shift from sovereign power, demonstrated grandly yet sporadically through public torture and execution, to an enduring and less visible form of disciplinary power (Rouse 2007). Rather than acting top-down, disciplinary power permeates day-to-day living, acting through and being performed by individuals, whom Foucault terms 'vehicles of power'. Disciplinary power makes knowledge and power inseparable, resulting in discourses of power-knowledge. According to Foucault, as 'vehicles of power' no individual is outside of the system of power-knowledge, rather systems (which he describes as carceral and Panoptic) create self-surveying, confessing and docile bodies (technologies of the self) which gaze upon the bodies of others whilst simultaneously surveying themselves.

Discourses of power-knowledge, left unchallenged, become false 'truths' (Stein 2010), or, as Titchkosky (2000) puts it, 'official textbooks'. 'Official textbooks' of disability tell us that disabled bodies are abnormal, and should be regarded less highly than 'normal', 'able bodies' (J. Butler 1993; Hughes, Russell and Paterson 2005). By casting disabled people as Other, 'official textbooks' of disability work through a disciplining 'gazing' culture to ensure we keep a *particularly* careful eye on problematic disabled bodies (Biggs and Powell 2001; Hughes 2005; Shildrick 1997). Foucault (1977) tells us that this gaze does not just come from doctors and others within the medical profession. Rather, we are all expected to gaze upon 'abnormal' bodies. 'Physical difference [...] makes the bodies of disabled people public property' (Barton 1993: 243).

Hughes (2001) points to dependency as another untrue 'truth' in the textbook of disability. The dependency/disability story goes as follows: disability is a deficiency, an abnormality, a biological fact. This deficiency is a tragedy that leaves disabled people dependent and in need of care. Thus, '[t]he 'invalid' [the wrongly constituted disabled person] is a fiscal burden but one who deserves the support and succour of the community' (Hughes 2001: 24). Garthwaite (2011) highlights that Cameron understands this story when he states that: 'if people "really cannot work", then they will be looked after' (Cameron cited in Garthwaite 2011: 370). The message here is one of disability as a tragedy. It is only reasonable, only humane, to be charitable towards those less fortunate than ourselves. If my imagined conversation with a minister was to continue, he may recount to me that his problem, I must understand, is not with those who are *really* disabled, but those who are masquerading as disabled, those not-really disabled people, taking us ordinary, reasonable people for a ride. I get it now! 'Oh', I exclaim, 'how reasonable of you, minister – now I really do see what a reasonable man you are! You just want to locate those unreasonable others!' … but then it dawns on me,

'… but, minister, 'how are *we*' – (yes, *we*: me and the minister, we are now a *we*, an *us*, united against *them* – he has convinced me that *they*, the not-really or not-disabled-enough disabled people, are the Other, not me) – 'how are *we* going to separate the two? How do *we* find out who's *really* disabled?' Luckily for me, the minister has the answer, 'simply, Miss Slater, through the increasingly penetrating welfare gaze'.

Perhaps now even the imagined reality of my story is becoming less imaginable. The minister is himself drawing on Foucault, but Foucault would dispute the minister's conscious compliance in any process of gaze, as, part of the doctrine of 'governmentality' is that it renders bodies docile in the process of self-governance. Hence, power is made invisible (Giroux 2009; Rouse 2007). Let us continue imagining, however, long enough to ponder what is happening in my dialogue with the minister. Firstly, what does the minister mean when he talks of the 'welfare gaze'? With the welfare gaze comes an expectation of self-governance. Those accessing welfare services are expected to assess and govern themselves through self-assessment processes. In coalition policy there is a focus on young people aspiring to reach (neo)liberally productive and 'independent' 'adult' lives (Department for Education 2013). Yet, in contrast, in order to access benefits and services disabled people must prove they are 'disabled enough' by filling in forms declaring what they *cannot* do. Ironically, with less access to welfare and benefits, the form increases in volume and length, and the expectation of self-surveillance is heightened. Question 36 of the DLA form asked: 'Do you usually have difficulty or need help with your toilet needs?' (Department of Works and Pensions 2009: 18). On answering 'yes' the claimant is required to go into further detail: how often do you need help? For how long? Do you struggle to concentrate and need motivating with your toilet needs? How often? For how long? Shildrick explains this process as such:

> In focusing on singular behaviour, the state-sponsored model of disability promotes individuals failing above any attention to environmental factors. The DLA pack rigidly constructs and controls the definitional parameters of what constitutes disability in such a way that those who need to place themselves within that definition are obliged to take personal responsibility in turning a critical gaze upon their own bodies … power/knowledge relies on self-surveillance. (Shildrick 1997: 51)

'Disability' is thus produced as a social fact of 'tragedy', 'burden' and 'charity', outside of a socio-cultural and political context. One of the contexts within which the discourse of disability is produced is through a culture of suspicion, in which disabled people and their allies must prove their right to support by writing about their 'health, demeanour, comportment or behaviour in terms of culturally acceptable disability discourses' rather being able to 'offer more enabling alternatives' (Goodley and Runswick-Cole 2011b: 62). For Goodley and Runwick-Cole (2011b: 62), this amounts to psycho-emotional violence which 'undermines the emotional well-being of disabled people and can be just as disabling as structural barriers' (Reeve 2002: 493). The reality of this psycho-emotional violence for disabled young people becomes clear in the later chapters of this book. Furthermore, the Scope (Boffey 2011) report alerts us that on top of psycho-emotional violence, representations of disabled people as scroungers mean an increase in what Goodley and Runswick-Cole term 'real' violence:

> Real violence is experienced physically and psychologically. [...] The real of violence is an embodied encounter: of pain inflicted by one body on another. [...] real physical encounters with violence; pain, humiliation and, we could suggest, torture. (Goodley and Runswick-Cole 2011b: 606)

Conclusions

With the above in mind, it is perhaps unsurprising that disability studies researchers continually evoke 'neoliberalism' as a context within which disabled people do not fare well. Nor is it surprising that disability studies researchers and disabled activists have attempted to rewrite and challenge the 'official textbook' of disability. The point of this chapter, however, has been to explore how 'liberal' arguments of 'sameness' and 'equality' can soon slip into the demonising 'neoliberal' rhetoric of personal responsibility. Both presume a 'normatively *dis*embodied political subject' (Sothern 2007: 147, original italics). As we are all presumed to be inherently 'the same' any suffering is blamed upon individual deficit and the ideal figure of adulthood normativity (Mr Reasonable, if you will) remains invisibly pedestalled and unproblematised.

Furthermore, we have also seen that the 'reasonable' face given through Cameron's (neo)liberal Big Society discourse puts disabled people in danger. Liberal arguments of 'equality' are taken in and pacified through inadequate legislation. Mr Reasonable's boundaries may expand a little to include a few willing/able to fit into his reasonable ways of being. Yet, through this, the exclusion of many more is justified; indeed, exclusion is rendered reasonable. Rather the bearers of rights, the 'reasonableness' of (neo)liberalism makes (some) disabled people recipients of charity (Runswick-Cole and Goodley 2011). Yet, it also leads to a violent, scapegoating culture where we are all expected to watch out for the fakes in the system. Many others are left out in the cold.

Although some may manage to dwell in the cracks, ultimately (neo)liberalism gives us two options: fit into Mr Reasonable's reasonable ways of being; or fight for survival. It is for this reason that I will, for the remainder of the book, follow Sothern (2007) in employing the term '(neo)liberalism' to capture the context I am researching and writing within. Chapter 2 will interrogate (neo)liberal discourses around 'youth' further. Here, we will see more clearly that both the 'liberal' and the 'neoliberal' rely upon a sameness of being which do not allow for the multiplicities of ways to be/come. Rather young people are expected to become (neo)liberal adults (Mr Reasonables). The thesis of Chapter 2 will thus be this: what if, rather than challenging disability's positioning as 'outside' discourses of youth and adulthood, we instead challenge the whole notion of a (neo)liberal adult? This gauntlet is taken up in Chapters 3 to 6.

Chapter 2

Youth as Border Zone, Disability and Disposability (or, Challenging Youth as Becoming-Reasonable Adult)

I explained in the last chapter that I follow Sothern (2007) in employing the term (neo)liberalism. My argument for this was that both 'neoliberal' arguments of personal responsibility and 'liberal' arguments of equity based on 'sameness', pedestal a certain type of person, (or adult) at the expense of others. Chapter 2 furthers this discussion by thinking more specifically about how this relates to youth and youth research. I will argue that as young people are considered becoming-adults, what we mean by 'adulthood' impacts upon our conceptualisations of youth (Slater 2013a). In fact, I'll argue that the ideal (neo)liberal subject is inherently adult. Confusingly, however, to be the (neo)liberal adult one must also hold onto certain parts of youthful discourse, and discard others (Slater 2012b, 2013a). I use this chapter, therefore, to unpick this complicated 'adulthood ideal' further.

To do this I draw on Lesko's (2012) idea of youth as a 'border zone' between child and adult. Rather than assume youth (or 'adolescence') as a scientific and therefore neutral stage of human development, Lesko (2012) argues that we need to put the emergence of adolescent discourse into a historical, socio-cultural and political context. Scholars have been influenced by Foucault's (1977) work around 'discourse' and 'technologies', and through this helped us to see that developmental discourse has a purpose particular to a time and place (Burman 2008a; Lesko 2012; Morss 1996; Walkerdine 1993). I therefore argue that considering youth as policed border zones of technologies, which aim to create a certain subject of (neo)liberal adulthood, can be useful in theorising the lived-experiences of young dis/abled people. These 'technologies' are then unpicked, with the help of the young disabled people I spent time with, over Chapters 3 to 6.

I begin by considering disability studies research around 'youth'. Here I find that disability studies accounts rarely engage with more critical studies of 'youth' (Slater 2013b). Rather a liberal argument of sameness sets disabled young people up as 'becoming-adult' (just like everybody else). I also find, however, that neither do critical accounts of 'youth', engage with 'disability'. I therefore consider how a (neo)liberal 'adult' ideal impacts upon not only discourses of 'youth', but also, 'disability'. Drawing on Giroux's (2009) insights into 'disposable youth' within (neo)liberalism, I will argue that the (neo)liberal rule of the coalition government threatens young disabled people not meeting the 'adult ideal' with disposability. Thus, I once again call for a theoretical engagement that considers disabled young people outside liberal youth-as-becoming-adult discourse.

Disabled Youth in Research

In the previous chapter I considered liberal equality-based arguments of 'sameness' and argued that there is a danger of such arguments playing into the hands of neoliberal doctrine. We can see such arguments being used in some recent disability studies research around disabled young people. Through a rhetoric of 'sameness' we are told that young disabled people are no different from their non-disabled peers. Hendry and Pascall (2002: 732), for example, argue that disabled young people aspire to 'achieve adulthood through employment, to gain resources for independent living in their own choice of housing, wider social networks, escape from poverty, and a sense of contributing to society'. Morris (2002: 7) is not alone when she highlights that 'sex and sexuality figure as important issues in the transition to adulthood for non-disabled young people but adults do not always recognise that disabled young people will have the same sexual feelings as others of their age. This can result in a lack of information and in inappropriate advice, creating confusion for young people, their parents and carers'.

All the above arguments imply that young disabled people have the same aspirations as their non-disabled peers, but material and attitudinal barriers make it harder for them to meet adulthood aspirations such as employment, independence and sexual relations. On the surface, there is nothing inherently 'wrong' with these arguments. They, in fact, appear reasonable. As will be considered further in Chapters 3 to 6, disabled people are often rooted in infantilising discourses and practices we may associate with childhood (Baron, Riddell and Wilson 1999). Through employing an argument of 'sameness' therefore, disability studies scholars are positing young disabled people as becoming-adults, just like their non-disabled peers. The only difference, they tell us, between disabled and non-disabled young people, is that for disabled young people structural and attitudinal barriers hinder them in reaching the markers of 'adulthood'. Morris (2002: 10) notes, for example, that service providers should 'recognise that transition is a process, rather than a series of assessments and reviews; and that disabled young people's transition to adulthood may well take longer – because of the barriers they face – than that of their non-disabled peers'. One way of removing such barriers is through service provision which young people themselves should be in control of (Hendey and Pascall 2002; Morris 1999, 2002; Rabiee, Priestley and Knowles 2001).

I engage with these kinds of arguments in Chapter 3. For now, however, I want to highlight something puzzling: that there is a need to assert that the aspirations of disabled young people are similar to those of their non-disabled peers is telling. It speaks of the general assumption that to be disabled is to be different – should we be surprised that disabled and non-disabled young people have similar hopes and dreams? Non-disabled and disabled young people are watching the same television programmes; reading the same magazines; listening to the same radio stations. They are therefore being delivered the same message that to be successful is to meet up to adulthood expectation. In fact, the message of adulthood normativity may be delivered to disabled young people (and others that it is worried are less likely to meet convention) louder and stronger (Kelly 2006). Scholars have noted that although young people's priorities tend to be 'here-and-now' experiences of fun and friendships, even *leisure* services for disabled youth focus on 'learning life skills, increasing independence and/or self-esteem' (Murray 2002: 1) and preparing for a 'meaningful life without work' (Priestley 2003: 91). Add to this an 'overcoming' or 'supercrip' narrative of disability (Barnes 1992; Deal 2003; Rousso 2013), and we understand that disabled young people may feel the pressure to meet up to adulthood expectation more than their non-disabled peers in order to 'prove themselves' (discussed further in Chapter 3). As Gordon and Lahelma (2002: 2) write, becoming-adult (for, it seems, both disabled and non-disabled young people) means achieving 'independence, achieved through separation from parents, financial self-sufficiency and establishment of heterosexual relations' (see also, Slater 2013a). Whereas the message for some young people is that this 'adulthood' is achievable, for others 'adulthood' is not considered a realistic goal. Disability studies scholars tend to rely on a liberal argument that disabled young people are 'no different than anybody else' so that they are not positioned outside the 'youth-as-becoming-adult' mantra.

Through Gordon and Lahelma's (2002) (de)construction of adulthood, however, we begin to see problems emerging. We have already begun to problematise a heterosexual expectation through the previous two chapters. As I consider further in Chapter 6, although an assertion that disabled young people have 'the same sexual feelings as others of their age' (Morris 2002: 6) may counter a narrative of asexuality that surrounds disability (Kim 2011), it fails to acknowledge the problematic nature of conflating all young people's sexual desires as 'the same'. Furthermore, we saw in the previous chapter that the liberal mantra of things (anything) being 'one's own business' a) assumes us to be 'free', 'independent' and 'autonomous' (Erevelles 1996); b) creates particular power dynamics; and c) relies on certain assumptions, concerning the public/private divide. Moreover, such a liberal mantra of 'one's own business' is reflected in liberal becoming-adult discourse: the expectation to leave the dependency of childhood and become-independent-adult (discussed further in Chapter 4).

Ferguson and Ferguson (2001) point out that assumptions of becoming-dependent can be harmful when we consider young disabled people's often interconnected lives. They reflect on parenting their disabled son, Ian, who, 'over the years has collected a variety of labels' (Ferguson and Ferguson 2001: 71). As Ian requires assistance and support, they feel a Western pedestalling of independence leads to the devaluing of his life. For them, there is a therefore vicious irony in fighting for their son's inclusion within a construction of 'adulthood independence' when it is this very construct that has led to his exclusion. They are therefore left pondering about how to best to support their disabled son:

> Do we emphasize his differences and try to avoid the conclusions of inferiority that society has traditionally attached, or do we emphasize his sameness and risk perpetuating the same social rules and expectations that have already unfairly excluded him? Should Ian's adulthood look the same or different from the dominant cultural models, or from any alternative models presented by other parts of the disability community? (Ferguson and Ferguson 2001: 87)

For the Fergusons (2001), the liberal argument we see projected above – that disabled young people are 'just the same as everybody else' – means positioning their son within a discourse of normative adulthood, which denies him a host of experiences and alternative ways of becoming as a disabled person. They begin to alert us to the ableism of adulthood, that liberal arguments of 'sameness' leave unproblematised – I will think again in Chapter 3 about how this dynamic played out in the lives of young disabled people I spent time with. For now though, I ask this: what is this 'adulthood' we implicitly speak of? And why is it that disability studies researchers are so concerned to fight for young disabled people's place within it? Let us consider 'youth' and 'adulthood' more critically.

Conceptualising 'Youth': From 'Development' to 'Border Zone'

If age is a 'biological reality', then 'youth' or, to use the term used more often with 'scientific' frameworks, 'adolescence', is simply a way of constituting a population based upon this 'reality' (Slater 2013a). This was the idea expressed by many developmental psychologists working in the 'normative period' of developmentalism at the turn of the twentieth century (Berk 2010). In the last chapter, however, we began to see that what we are expected to do and be is dependent upon wider socio-cultural and political contexts. The problem with an assumption of 'biological reality', therefore, is that we miss an important analysis of the time and place within which these ideas are formed. Perhaps thinking more broadly around youth research can alert us to why disability studies researchers are so keen to assert disabled young people as becoming-adults, 'like everybody else'. To do this, we need to go back to the late 1800s and early 1900s.

Granville Stanley Hall, sometimes referred to as the 'father of adolescence', was a psychologist working at the turn of the twentieth century. Hall (1904) grounded studies in evolutionary ideas, and through this, he generated norms and averages which he claimed represented 'typical development' (Berk 2010; Burman 2008b). As people interested in disability studies, alarm bells are perhaps already ringing: an assumption of a 'norm' can prove dangerous to those not fitting into these (socially-constructed) categories, such as disabled people. Hall is perhaps most famous for developing the 'storm and stress' model of adolescence. He attempted to explain the (continually) prevailing view of young people as rebellious and irresponsible by arguing that adolescence was a period of turbulence which paralleled human 'development' from 'savages' into 'civilised beings'. This theory, known as recapitulation theory, paralleled the growth of each individual child with the development of human kind (Lesko 1996: 149). Babies, children and adolescents were considered to be somewhere between 'pre-human', 'primitive' and 'man'; with 'man' (and the gendering is important to note) projected as the end point of 'civilisation' (Lesko 2002, 2012). The entwined racism, sexism, dis/ablism and other prejudice of evolutionary theory (see Burman 2008a, 2008b) was transferred to development theory; a threefold parallel developing where animals, 'savages' and children were all presumed as equal. For example, on posture, one author writes:

> [S]avage races do not stand so erect as civilised races. Country people ... tend to bend forward, and the aristocrat is more erect than the plebeian. In this respect women appear to be nearer to the infantile [and apelike] condition than men. (Serres cited in Lesko 1996: 140)

Although the overt prejudice of the above may appear shocking, at the time (like now) science was valued highly. As Hall's work was situated within a scientific paradigm his theories were largely undisputed and helped to produce 'adolescence' as a 'fact of life' that came, for all of us, between child and adult. Moreover, although the science behind it may have been critiqued, that 'adolescence' is a stage of life we all go through remains relatively undisputed today (Lesko 2012). The 'facts' of 'child', 'youth' and 'adult' are rarely disputed. Disability studies scholars, we saw earlier, fight for young disabled people's place as 'adults'. Furthermore, like we saw in relation to 'disability' in the last chapter, each stage of 'development' has its own 'official textbook' (Titchkosky 2003). The battle disability studies scholars are sometimes fighting is for disabled people to have a place in the 'textbook of adulthood'. The question I ask in this chapter is what such an endeavour entails.

Lesko (2012) draws on Foucault to argue that we need to consider how histories relate to current day theory. This illuminates that turn of the century theories about 'adolescence' are not purely historical, but continuing to influence the way we think about young people today. For example, neurologists have been the latest group to scientifically study 'adolescence'. Such studies are in their early stages yet they have nevertheless been used to justify the implementation of policy (Payne 2010). Payne (2010) argues that the reason for this trend is that neurological studies fit with earlier recapulation theories. Although much critiqued within sciences, social sciences and other disciplines, early nineteenth-century studies continue to dominate the ways in which we think about youth. Overtly illustrating this, in 2012 a *BBC News* headline read 'Brain scan study to understand workings of teenage mind' (Ghosh 2013a, 2013b). Although not mentioned in the news clip itself, the website accompanying the BBC report explains Hall's evolutionary model of adolescence, not as historical, but as current theory. Proclaiming that:

'every individual rehearses the evolutionary history of their species'.

'... emotions arise from more primitive brain regions and so according to this theory they develop more quickly than higher, more rational brain functions as a person grows up'.

'the human brain [... is] carrying a lot of evolutionary baggage – which may be at the root of the difficulties of the teenage years'. (Ghosh 2013b)

To challenge such an argument, rather than accept 'adolescence' as a scientific 'truth' Lesko (2012) traces and contextualises the beginnings of adolescent discourse. She highlights that the turn of the twentieth century in America (where Hall was working) saw a rise in disciplines such as anthropology, psychology and pedagogy. These disciplines positioned themselves as scientific, and therefore 'truthful' and 'objective'. Yet, these scientists weren't working in vacuums. Rather, they were working in a context where there were worries about America's nationhood and manhood. As youth was considered to be the apex of human development, young people embodied the potential to fulfil the colonial dreams of America. Yet, there was also a risk: if young people failed at meeting the desired outcomes, they were thought to threaten the wellbeing of the nation.

Again drawing on Foucault, Lesko (2012) argues that the entwining of theories, policies and practices which aimed to carve young people into the desired adult citizen worked as 'technologies of adolescence'. In Foucauldian terms, a 'technology' is about more than what we may deem to be 'technological' in day-to-day conversation (computers, iPhones, and so on). Rather, by technologies of adolescence Lesko (2012: 58) means 'the techniques of naming, studying, diagnosing, predicting, and administering an identifiable adolescent population'. In other words, a technology of adolescence refers to the processes that work together to define 'adolescence' (and 'adolescents'), produce what may *appear* to be the 'fact' of adolescence, or create a discourse or textbook of adolescence, thereby creating certain patterns and expectations for the governance of youth.

Both today and at the turn of the nineteenth century, this discourse of adolescence revolves around the biological assumption of 'becoming-adult' (Slater 2013a). Lesko (2002, 2012), however, points out that the adult citizen desired by American psychologists at this time was both raced (white), and gendered (with the majority of study concentrating on boys). Thus, technologies of adolescence became the rationale for boys' education aiming 'to produce young, masculine, Christians' (Lesko 2002: 183) who would work for the good of the nation. Policies and practices worked in particular raced and gendered ways. There was a general consensus, for example, that educators needed to aim to create 'more manly boys and more womanly girls' (Lesko 2012: 66). One way of doing this was to encourage boys to take part in team sports. However, as teamwork was considered to be 'a form of association rooted in the heritage of the Anglo-Saxon 'race', it was thought that team sport would 'come naturally to Anglo-Saxon youth but could uplift others if they were educated to it' (Lesko 2012: 66). In other words, team play was considered a way to make non-Anglo-Saxon boys 'more manly', and with this were connotations of being 'more white'. Girls on the other hand, were dealt with separately:

> To coax boys to stay in school, high school administrators offered a well-organized, competitive sports program run by rugged men, and channelled girls into cheerleading. (Lesko 2012: 67)

Lesko helps us to see that despite being portrayed as scientific (and therefore supposedly objective and neutral), youth and adulthood are produced as social 'facts' functioning within a particular context. Rather than an implicit stage of human development, she posits 'youth' as 'in border zones between the imagined end points of adult and child' (Lesko 2012: 42). Border zones of youth function, through schools, families youth services and so on to shape children, in particular identity-dependent ways, to meet the social, cultural and political adulthood requirements of that particular time and place. We know from Chapter 1 that the time and place we are thinking about in this book is what Peck and Tickell (2002: 380) call the 'heartlands of neoliberal discursive production, North America and Western Europe'. Furthermore, the raced and gendered adult subject also emerges in adult discourse today.

Feminist scholars have noted that whereas men are considered 'whole' (and therefore adult), women are considered incomplete and infantilised as 'childlike' (Burman 2008b). Just as Lesko notes that policy at the turn of the century focused on boys' education, some contemporary educationists have argued that the panic induced when girls overtook boys in school league tables in Australia, the USA and Britain from the 1990s onwards, highlights the unrepresentative importance put on boys' compared to girls' education (Mills and Keddie 2007). Critical race theorists and activists have similarly pointed out that the Western values of white people, such as autonomy and independence, are valued above those such as community and interdependence, which are traditionally recognised by some people of colour (Lorde 2007). Furthermore, it has been argued that the education of black young people (specifically boys) often focuses on containment, rather than a meaningful learning experience (Giroux 2009; Ladson Billings 2011; Watts and Erevelles 2004). Thus, it is not only the early twentieth century, but also the contemporary Western twenty-first-century adult subject that must embody characteristic of both 'whiteness' and 'masculinity'.

You may have noticed through our discussion of 'youth' thus far, however, that there is a lack of attention to dis/ability. Lesko (2012: 11–12) acknowledges that there is limited focus on sexuality in her work. Yet, there is no mention of her missing analysis of dis/ability. Of course, all studies have limitations. It is important to note, for example, that this book offers an analysis focused on the minority world, with limited attention paid to 'race' over Chapters 3 to 6. However, that dis/ability is not mentioned as a limitation alongside the others in Lesko's book, tells us about the lack of attention disability has been paid within critical studies of youth. Furthermore, Lesko's missing analysis of dis/ability becomes even more conspicuous we note the impetus put on young people's 'health' at the turn of the century. Creating a healthy generation of young adults was considered key to a physically productive workforce who would be able to fight for their country. Furthermore, 'health' was not only about the 'efficient functioning of body parts', but also linked to morals:

> Health is the condition of all success and nothing can atone for its loss. The art of keeping our bodies always to the very top of their condition is thus the art of arts in which so many science culminate … The muscles are the only organs of the will, and have done all the work man has accomplished in the world … All exercises that strengthen and enlarge muscles strengthen and enlarge the brain fibres or cells. (Hall in Lesko 2012: 47)

We realise from the above that, despite Lesko's (2012) lack of attention to dis/ability, 'ability' (frequently operationalised through a discourse of 'health') was a key feature of the late nineteenth century becoming-adult population. The tying of 'morals', 'health' and 'ability' is also apparent in children's fiction at the time. Citing examples such *What Katy Did* and *Jack and Jill*, Dowkey (2004) points out that in late nineteenth- and early twentieth-century children's literature, disability emerges as a punishment or lesson in consciousness and morals that 'is not cured purely by a change of heart, but *is* a means of spiritual discipline'. Furthermore, in such tales children 'rarely become disabled adults: either they die young, or experience a miracle cure' (Dowkey 2004). The message around disability we are delivered from these texts is that one cannot be both 'grownup' and 'disabled'; disability is equated with a childlike way of being.

Once again, it is important to not write the above off only as historical disablism. Disabled people today remain rooted in childhood discourse. Baron et al. (1999) for example, tell us about 43-year-old Clare who is so busy in the week with the 'leisure' activities imposed upon her, that she only has time for her preferred paid employment during weekends. Furthermore, the linking of 'bodily ideals' and morals also remains pervasive. Children are taught in classrooms, for example, to 'control' their bodies by sitting still and obeying the teacher's instructions (James 2000). There is little space for some dis/abled children's pleasures of rocking and flapping hands (Goodley and Runswick-Cole 2010). As I have pointed out elsewhere:

> The 'good' student in the classroom has the body that walks properly, sits up straight, does not fidget, ties its shoelaces and tucks in its shirt; the older the child, the higher the expectation to have a 'good' classroom body. [The] process of judging the interior of the body by its exterior begin[s] in school, and children are aware of this. Discourses of 'good' bodies work alongside ableist discourses of 'normal' and 'healthy' bodies, and, through these discourses, children learn the cultural importance of bodywork. (Slater 2012b)

Like they did at the turn of the twentieth century, technologies at border zones of youth today function to ensure that the child meet the requirements of the twenty-first century (neo)liberal adult. This means moving, not from the 'developmental fact' of 'childhood' to the 'developmental fact' of 'adulthood', but from a socially constructed discourse of 'childhood' to a socially constructed discourse of 'adulthood'. Such a discourse associates the child with femininity, asexuality, emotions, dependency and a lack of productivity, to a pedestalled discourse of adulthood associated with masculinity, sexuality, rationality, civilisation, independence and productivity (Burman 2008a: 2008b; Slater 2013a). Furthermore, we will see as this chapter and the book continues, that the twenty-first century (neo)liberal adult subject is inherently 'able' (Runswick-Cole and Goodley 2011; Slater 2013a). I want to turn now to consider more carefully how border zones of youth function in (neo)liberal Britain.

(Neo)liberal ~~Disabled~~ Youth-as-Becoming-Adult

Giroux (2009) argues that an increasingly (neo)liberal context means a shift in perceptions of young people within a discourse of paternalism and protection, to one of 'personal responsibility'. Giroux is writing in an American context. However, his arguments also resonate when we consider UK politics and policy. As well as the changes to disability services and benefits outlined in Chapter 1, since the arrival of the coalition government young people have faced the lessening of both formal and informal educational opportunities. These include:

- The end of *Educational Maintenance Allowance* (a weekly grant to support young people in further education).

- A tripling of tuition fees in higher education.

- Cuts of £819 million to children's services (2011–12 figures). With schools' funding ring-fenced, effects of children's service cuts were arguably felt most greatly by young people (Butler 2011).

- In Sheffield, for example, youth service faced a 46% reduction in staff, and an £8m budget slashed to £4.6m. This meant the number of youth clubs went from 41 in 2010, to 23 in 2013 (Pidd 2013).

Such a shift seems akin to Giroux's (2009) fear: young people are no longer a generation worth nurturing and investing in. Considering such a climate in relation to Lesko's (2012) 'technologies of youth' (which educational institutions are implicated within), however, we could come to a slightly different conclusion. We may assume that with a (neo)liberal rhetoric of 'freedom', the technology of youth is disbanded. A (neo)liberal trope would tell us that young people have the freedom, outside of technologies, to become in a multiplicity of ways. We saw in Chapter 1 though that (neo)liberalism is complex, contradictory and pervasive (Larner 2003; Peck and Tickell 2002; Sothern 2007). Considering media discourse following the 'riots' taking place in major cities across England in August 2011 can help us to see this.

The (so-called) 'riots' of Summer 2011 saw some (mainly) young people take to the streets (Smith 2011). There is no denying that both property and people were damaged. Contrary to most mainstream media reports, however, this damage was caused by both 'rioters' *and* police. Furthermore, despite the harsh climates young people were living in, both during and after the riots, most reports failed to contextualise young people's actions in the uncertain futures they were facing. Rather, a picture was painted of an uncontrollable 'mindless mob'

(Cavanagh and Dennis 2012). Young people were seen as a 'risk'. Similarly to his justifications for *The Big Society* we saw in Chapter 1, for Prime Minister David Cameron the riots were a result of:

> Irresponsibility. Selfishness. Behaving as if your choices have no consequences. Children without fathers. Schools without discipline. Reward without effort. Crime without punishment. Rights without responsibilities. Communities without control. Some of the worst aspects of human nature tolerated, indulged – sometimes even incentivised – by a state and its agencies that in parts have become literally de-moralised. (Cameron in Stratton 2011)

As the initial aftermath of the riots passed, a variety of alternative opinions began to emerge about how to respond to the riots. Some commentators from the political left noted that the majority of young people involved were poor young people of colour, that many of the youth services previously on offer to them were either under threat or no longer in existence, and that the job market was unstable (Smith 2011). For Cameron, however, the insistence was that, during the years Labour was in power, too much responsibility had been removed from the individual and shifted onto the state. A commentary in *The Guardian* was typical in its claim that the riots were a result of 'allow[ing] our welfare system to prop up immoral lifestyles' (Bailey 2011). The author claimed that, '[w]e have not taught young people that entitlement culture is wrong'. The familiar (neo)liberal trope was that young people needed to take personal responsibility for their actions. In the spirit of *The Big Society*, the morning after the riots, Boris Johnson, mayor of London, took to the streets; urging people to join him for a *Big Society* clean up and take responsibility for their own communities. Like Giroux (2009) warns, however, Cameron's main focus was to seek out and punish the ring leaders. Prisons became a key part of the technology of youth Cameron was advocating, as his (neo)liberal solution to the problem of youth, was to contain until (and perhaps beyond) adulthood.

Another entwined dominant post-riot discourse deemed young people an entitled generation who were obsessed with commodity (Brand 2011). Russell Brand, celebrity/presenter/political commentator, was amongst those who pointed out the hypocrisy of this:

> That state of deprivation though is, of course, the condition that many of those rioting endure as their unbending reality. No education, a weakened family unit, no money and no way of getting any. JD Sports [a UK sports shop] is probably easier to desecrate if you can't afford what's in there and the few poorly paid jobs there are taken. Amidst the bleakness of this social landscape, squinting all the while in the glare of a culture that radiates ultraviolet consumerism

and infrared celebrity. That daily, hourly, incessantly enforces the egregious, deceitful message that you are what you wear, what you drive, what you watch and what you watch it on, in livid, neon pixels. The only light in their lives comes from these luminous corporate messages. No wonder they have their fucking hoods up. (Brand 2011)

Similarly to Brand, Giroux (2009) marks (neo)liberal society as a consumer society. He notes that in the consuming society, the rights of the citizen are replaced by the rights of the consumer. He in fact maintains that you cannot be a citizen without being a consumer. For Brand, therefore, it was no surprise that 'the riots' meant the looting of stuff (which included not only designer brands, but also everyday grocery items) by people who couldn't afford to 'consume' in the pedestalled sense. Giroux (2009) goes one step further. He argues that the commodification of products has turned into the commodification of human beings: a country's success measured through Gross National Product; children encouraged to be entrepreneurial; the 'active citizen' not active at all, unless this activity happens within markets (Giroux 2009). The perceived 'value' of a human being equates to their market-value: 'in the society of consumers, no one can become a subject without first turning into a commodity' (Bauman cited in Giroux 2009: 31). The consumer society is a fast-paced society with a fast-turnover of goods: we no longer value products of quality that will last, but want cheap, one-off products that we expect to quickly dispose of. He maintains in fact that consumption is not about possessions at all, but about disposing of them. And, when people become commodities, people too are disposable.

Youth, Activity, Passivity and Disposability

I find it useful at this point to think about young people's actions in term of discourses of activity and passivity; as there are some strange contradictions playing out here. On the one hand, we see young people positioned as lazy, passive and unproductive; yet, on the other hand, young people are demonised for their dangerous over-activity (I think about this more in relation to disabled young people in Chapter 5). Foucault's (1979) theory of 'bio-power' can help us to work through such contradiction. 'For Foucault, the human subject in modernity is constituted by disciplinary techniques of bio-power which structure, produce and optimise the capabilities of the body, enhancing its economic utility and ensuring its political docility' (Hughes and Paterson 1997: 332). In 'bio-political' systems, power-knowledge works through bodies and, rather than 'free' to make 'choices' (as (neo)liberal doctrine would have us believe), bodies are rendered economically productive, yet politically docile.

This distinction between economic productivity and political docility explains what at first seems a strange paradox; in a system that renders bodies docile and dependent, young people are encouraged to meet up to the ideal of an active, independent, neoliberal subject.

For Giroux (2009), therefore, the lessening of state power is a façade. What we are left with is a change of relations: the welfare state becomes the market state, and the state/citizen relationship becomes one of corporate/consumer. The state does not lose its power, but reconfigures it. We are no longer citizens of the state, but customers of the market, and, like the customer entering a shop, we have a choice … but the choice has to be made out of what is already on the shelves and considered in relation to the money we already have in our pocket. To be politically active in order to change the system is not a choice on offer. Rather, '[t]he "active citizen" is the employed individual who, whilst committed to the pursuit of economic well-being, seeks to do good to others, but purely in a private capacity' (Barton 1993: 244).

Barton above extrapolates (neo)liberalism's bias towards a charity model of disability which we began to unpack in Chapter 1. Advocates of (neo)liberalism maintain that the 'deserving poor' and the 'real needy' will be looked after as prosperity generated from the markets is passed down through acts of private do-goodery. Thus, the state is rendered unnecessary. What we have already seen, however, is that far from weakening its power, those in power rather brandish power in different market-led ways. The story of (neo)liberalism justifies such power through a rhetoric of 'custom' and 'choice' (Giroux 2009). The story goes as such: we all have a choice which we follow up with an action. Actions have consequences. As the consequence is only a result of individual choice, it is only the individual that it to blame (Barber 2007; Barton 1993; Giroux 2009). Disability is considered a tragic biological fact (not a choice) and disabled people therefore require charity (Barton 1993). However, there are the 'unreasonable' amongst us that claim to be, but are not really disabled, and these people need searching out (Garthwaite 2011). When the financial budget is in a state, it seems the number of (real) disabled people significantly decreases, and the number of those masquerading as disabled increases. These people, I maintain, are in danger of disposability.

Beyond Becoming-Reasonable-Adults

We begin to understand, therefore, why in such a hostile climate, disability studies researchers may be tempted to argue disabled young people are becoming-adult 'just the same as everybody else'. Border zones are dangerous (more so for some than others); and so too are border zones of youth. Arguably, when fighting for disabled young people's 'same' becoming-adultness, disability studies scholars are aiming to help them pass through the border zone, to the relative safety of adulthood. As I will come onto in a moment and expand upon in Chapter 3, sometimes for disabled young people and their advocates such a message is necessary in terms of survival. (Neo)liberalism, however, works in confusing and contradictory ways. Endeavouring to 'live-up-to' (neo)liberal normativity is therefore, is not easy (and often, not even possible).

The ideal young person, I conclude at the end of this chapter, is one striving, and on track to becoming, the (neo)liberal adult: the Mr Reasonable I addressed in my Preface. Key to this is a focus on entrepreneurialism. They must be economically active (spending within markets), but with an eye on future economic activity/productivity (future employment prospects). In order to achieve in the game of the entrepreneurs, they must be marketable. Ironically, popular on the market right now as features of the commodified subject are characteristics commonly paired with 'youthfulness': beauty, health, speed, fluidity (Slater 2012b). At the same time, however, they also need to be politically docile: to be grownup one must be compromising, conservative, moderate, rational and silent (Allen 1968; Burman 2008a). These juxtapose connotations of dangerously active, volatile young people that were portrayed during the riots (Slater 2012a). In current political climates those failing to meet the ideals of (neo)liberalism are left aside; the less-than-ideal human commodity disposed of.

Confusingly, however, the disabled person, (wrongly) construed as passive, is also one opposed to the ideal (neo)liberal adult subject (Giroux 2009; Kelly 2006). Looking back at history we should be wary. We have seen the rhetoric of 'the burden to society' used before with devastating consequences, at the time of Holocaust (Evans 2004). Giroux (2009: 2) deems (neo)liberal consumerism 'economic Darwinism'. I maintain, however, that representations of disabled people as dependent, despite having very real consequences, are by no means accurate representations. When it is taken into account that many of the cuts slash funding to the tools disabled people use to lead an 'independent' life (vehicles which allow them to get to work, personal assistance, and so on), the absurdity of such representation is illustrated.

The explorations made so far in this book, then, outline why I maintain that arguing that disabled young people are the same as their non-disabled peers does not go far enough in addressing dangerous discourses of (neo)liberal adulthood. Far from being neutral, discourses of both 'youth' and 'adulthood' work for the particular requirements of a time and place. As Wyn and White (1997: 94) point out, despite connotations of fluidity and change that surround 'youth', young people's transitions to adulthood involve 'choosing' from a few very set routes to adulthood. Furthermore, it is important to note that for some people, the choices on offer are fewer than for others. For some, there is no choice to meet up to the (neo)liberal ideal. The consequence for these people is either charity or disposability. As I argued in Chapter 1, although an argument of 'sameness' may mean some disabled young people are (reasonably, and often partially) included in the textbook of adulthood, many are rendered unreasonable. Any exclusion or marginalisation they face is therefore rendered reasonable, and they are left as part of a disposable population (Ferguson and Ferguson 2001; Giroux 2009; Sothern 2007; Titchkosky 2011).

Finally, to simply argue disabled young people are the 'same as everybody else' fails to recognise that disability offers us more than a choice from the menu. As Hughes (2001) points out, fighting for (and troubling our conceptions of) independence has been at the crux of disability activism. Under the rightist agenda, rather than being considered socially constituted, autonomy has been fetishised into some biologically inherent capacity; something you either do or do not have. For disabled youth, this is dangerous. In order to reposition dis/abled young people as active, a critique of the valued attributes of youth, adulthood, of the 'active citizen', of dependence and independence is vital.

Thus, when I say that arguing disabled young people are no different to anybody else is inadequate, it is not disabled young people's 'sameness' (or lack of it) which is problematic. Rather, my problem is with the normative imaginary of who this 'everybody else' is. I maintain that a (neo)liberally valued 'everybody else' can only exist at the expense of those whom it deems Other. It is for this reason that, through this book, I aim to turn the gaze back onto the conditions which allow for Mr Reasonable.

Conclusion

In the next chapter I will begin to introduce some stories from the young disabled people I spent time with during fieldwork. During my fieldwork, I certainly found resistance to, and struggles against, the societal positionings young disabled people were subject to – young disabled people were anything but passive. Yet, perhaps conversely at the end of this chapter, I found the young disabled people I spent time with were often demonstrating this resistance through themselves employing arguments of 'sameness' to combat disablist oppression. They told me that, like their peers, they wanted to be considered becoming-adults.

I keep this somewhat uncomfortable position in mind throughout the rest of the book. Bringing in the stories of young disabled people, the next chapter to an extent 'grounds' some of my discussion. Listening to young disabled people, their advocates and disabled activists helped me to think through when it is safe to reject an argument of 'sameness' (such I have justified the need for doing in this chapter), and when one needs to fight to be 'the same' for the sake of (often individual) survival. When we move onto Chapters 4, 5 and 6 we'll also see that disabled young people's fights through normative reasonable rhetoric often allowed them to lead lives that challenged the very terms they were employing. What the following chapters try to document, then, is how and whether we should be balancing short-term battles for survival, with longer-term unsettling projects of thinking 'otherwise' about 'youth', 'adulthood', 'dis/ability' – and, as we've seen – all the other identity positionings with which they are intertwined. I move into Chapter 3 now, to consider this by further interrogating the functioning of 'reason' at border zones of youth.

Chapter 3
The Making of Un/Reasonable Bodies at the Border Zone of Youth

rea.son.able

1 (to do [something]) fair, practical and sensible: **It is reasonable** to assume that he knew beforehand that this would happen. **Be reasonable!** We can't work late every night. Any reasonable person would have done exactly what you did. The prosecution has to prove **beyond reasonable doubt** that he is guilty of murder. **OPP[osite] unreasonable**.

(Hornby 2010: 1,266, original emphasis)

According to the *Oxford Advanced Learner's Dictionary* (Hornby 2010: 1,266), 'reason' is a 'cause of explanation for something that has happened or that someone has done'. *What is the reason that that happened? I want to know the reason you did that! We are not doing it for the simple reason that ...* The late seventeenth and early eighteenth centuries are sometimes known as The Age of Reason. During this time, intellectuals rejected tradition and culture in favour of scientific methods based upon reason. It is not surprising, then, that with reason there is an implication of logic and linearity. 'B' situation happened because of 'A' situation. Already, this seems out of kilter with the roundabout, no right-or-wrong, critical questioning conversations we've been having in this book so far. Yet although much of the time I spent with young disabled people involved critically questioning the world around us, there were other times that discussion was not the aim of the young people. Rather, the young people I spent time with wanted their arguments to both 'stand to reason' ['be clear to any sensible person who thinks about it' (Hornby 2010: 1,266)] and to be understood as *reasonable*, by the particular audience to whom their point was being aimed. Being understood as reasonable not only meant their point was taken more seriously, but also allowed them movement over the border zone of youth and into adulthood.

The relationships between reason, youth and disability are the focus of this chapter. Reason has been explained by philosophers as an attribute that one develops by becoming more autonomous through maturity (Code 2000; Kittay and Carlson 2010; Nagl-Docekal 1999). To prove oneself as adult, therefore, one must prove themselves 'reasonable'. Perhaps unsurprisingly given the conversations in Chapter 2, with this reason/adulthood entanglement comes of whole host of other expectations. As 'reason' is an attribute often positioned as oppositional to 'disability', particularly when impairments are perceived to do with the mind rather (or as well as) that the body (Kittay and Carlson 2010), one of these expectations is to be 'able'. To be considered 'unreasonable', as we will see, is to be considered outside of subjectivity, and this is dangerous. In this chapter, therefore, I will explore stories of 'reason' that emerged from my fieldwork from participants for whom appearing 'reasonable' meant being allowed movement over the border zone of youth. Without dismissing the immediacy of these projects (which were sometimes about survival), I'll argue that by linking reason with adulthood we maintain not only ableist and adultist norms, but also those intersecting with other forms of Otherness. I begin, however, by discussing the relationships between youth, disability, and becoming-adult.

Youth, Disability and Becoming-Adult

As outlined in the introductory chapter, one of my research settings was the Youth Forum (YF) of a disabled people's campaigning organisation. Here I conducted several workshops which were about imagining our best ever future worlds. I introduced the first 'futures workshop' at YF by asking young people to think of things which had annoyed them that week. Young people complained about the structural barriers they faced. Annoyances included 'inaccessible buses', 'taxis with high steps', 'inaccessible buildings' and 'badly made equipment'. Discussion for the majority of the session, however, revolved around how young disabled people were treated by others (mainly, non-disabled adults). Attitudinal annoyances included 'people telling you what to do', 'patronising attitudes' and 'people not treating you like an adult'. I asked the group how they thought these attitudes could be changed. The subsequent conversation went as follows:

Jenny: So how could we change people's attitudes ready for our best-ever future world?

Colin: Probably like doing outreach. Talking to people to help them understand.

Sarah: Getting your views across about what it really is to be a young disabled person so that they don't patronise you – education isn't it.

Jenny: And what would you tell them?

Colin: That we're no different from any other person and that we like to be treated equally.

Sarah: and want the same things.

(Transcript from first futures workshop with YF, 23rd November 2011)

Morris (2002: 11) writes that '[y]oung disabled people have the same aspirations as their non-disabled peers but require specific action to tackle the disabling barriers they experience'. Participants from YF agreed with Morris: there were strong views that people should know disabled people are 'no different from any other person'. They told me that they faced both physical and attitudinal barriers which meant they were treated differently to their non-disabled peers. Those around them failed to consider them as active becoming-adults.

As the workshop went on, stories of paternalism were shared between young people and youth workers. Fay, an actress in her 20s, talked about her drama group, where she is the only disabled person: 'people think I'm like 13 and they just look down at me like a kid and they won't let me do this and that'. The group discussed a colleague with 'restricted growth' at the organisation who gets 'treated like he's a seven-year-old child, nobody will believe him that he's a married guy with two kids and that he's a professional guy, an MBE!' A youth-worker shared the following:

I hate being treated like a 10 year old when I'm a 51 year old professional youth worker. This morning I had to be in dead early so I'm getting on the train at 6 o'clock and it's still pitch dark and I'm like that (sleepy face): 'where's the train?' And some guy comes up behind me and goes 'let's go, weeeeeeee! Whoopee! We'll soon have you away – honk!' I'm thinking – would you talk to another 51-year-old guy that's getting on a train like this?

To which two young people replied:

Fay: 'That's patronising!'

Gabby: 'It's stereotyping, without actually knowing you'.

(Transcript from first futures workshop with YF, 23rd November 2011)

We see the unquestioned ableism of adulthood rhetoric manifesting in everyday infantilising acts of mundane disablism. For the young people and their older disabled allies this was frustrating. Understandably, young people at YF thought disabled young people should be considered becoming-adults, just like their non-disabled peers. Young people wanted the freedom to try things out and carve their way to adulthood. Yet, they also explained to me that being allowed the same opportunities as their peers didn't just mean being 'like' their peers, but having to prove themselves above and beyond. Colin, a 23-year-old man, and regular attendee at YF, told a story that illustrated this well.

Before I met Colin from YF, a youth worker described him as having 'his fingers in a lot of pies'. After leaving college Colin became very involved in disability politics: fighting his own battles in relation to PAs and accessible housing, mentoring other young disabled people, and taking part in wider activism, on top of volunteering as a web designer for a local business. When I wished Colin a good weekend, he complained about how quiet weekends were, and that he could not wait for Monday. Murray (2002) notes that disabled young people's leisure time is likely to be spent engaged in solitary activities, such as playing on the computer. Colin's weekend pursuits reflected this. Colin was reliant on taxis for travel so was more mobile during the week because the disabled people's organisation and his workplace subsidised his transport. Weekends were lonely and boring. An interview between Colin and I went as follows:

Colin: 'I went to a conference and they said statistics have shown disabled people work more and aren't off sick as much as non-disabled people'.

Jenny: 'Do you think that's feeling you need to prove yourself? That you can't have a day off because they'll take any excuse to dismiss you?'

Colin: 'Yeah, no matter how ill I am I still struggle on'.

Jenny: 'I can imagine! Are you worried people will be like, it's 'cos he's a disabled person …'

Colin: 'Yeah. It hacks me off that people go out during the week, get absolutely hammered and then phone in sick the next day when there're people, disabled people out there, wanting to work and we can't get jobs. Recently, Philip Davis, the MP, said disabled people are scroungers … and that all the disability allowances get spent on trying to get things that non-disabled people have to work for – I don't agree'.

(Interview with Colin, 1st December 2011)

Colin's positive outlook meant he saw other people's low expectations as an opportunity to prove them wrong. Entering college, for example, he was told the course he later passed would be too stressful for him to cope with.

Colin had learnt to articulate himself through reasonable rhetoric in order to prove himself youth-as-becoming-adult, 'just like' his non-disabled peers. Yet, this did not simply mean being 'like' his non-disabled peers, but displaying a reasonableness which was above-and-beyond. Whilst his non-disabled peers sometimes took the opportunity to go on a night out, which meant going into work late/tired/hungover the next day, Colin felt unable to take such risks. He felt his employers already saw him as an (unreasonable) 'problem' and would take any opportunity to dismiss him. One very obvious and immediate consequence of not proving himself reasonably adult-enough to work would be to be physically restricted to his parental home. The choice was between forced dependency (akin to childhood), or self-disciplining adulthood responsibility – with little in between. Not being to be allowed to pass through the border zone of youth (Lesko 2012) could lead to paternalism and the denial of autonomy continuing into 'adulthood' (Baron, Riddell and Wilson 1999).

Ironically for Colin then, an argument of 'being just like everybody else' led not to the same freedoms as his non-disabled peers, but an adulthood responsibility and reasonableness not felt by many of his peers. A similar feeling emerged in a conversation between Freyja and the mother of Bjarne, a young man with intellectual impairments:

Mother: 'Bjarne was annoyed last night'.

Freyja: 'Oh dear, what about?'

Mother: 'I'm not sure. I kept asking him but never got to the bottom of it'.

Freyja: 'Sometimes we don't really know ourselves'.

Mother: 'Yeah but with Bjarne I constantly want a reason! Without a reason it's easy for other people to call it "challenging behaviour". I want to be able to say, "He's pissed off because you didn't let him choose his own dinner, you would be too!" … But he must get annoyed with my constant asking. I never do it with my other kids; they're allowed to just be moody teenagers'.

(My version of Freyja's conversation, based on notes
from research diary, 25th February 2012)

Bjarne's mother worries that rather than a 'moody teenager', Bjarne's 'unreasonable' moods would be read as a sign of his impairment (Mallett and Runswick-Cole 2012). Considered outside of normative developmental discourse, a label of 'challenging behaviour' has the potential to dominate

Bjarne's life (Crowe 2000). Therefore, Bjarne's mother felt she needed to argue Bjarne into a discourse of adulthood rationality and reasonableness in order to challenge the pathologisation of his 'bad mood' as an impairment-thing (Goodley and Runswick-Cole 2010). Yet, she also worried that through her actions she may be denying him the opportunity to 'be' a teenager in a bad mood; to live the 'unreasonableness' of youth.

Both Colin's and Bjarne's stories tell of resistance to an expectation of eternal childhood (Baron et al. 1999). Yet they also show that the structure, systems and ideologies this resistance plays out within can a) create a lack of space for disabled young people to 'be' young people; and b) allow them to 'become' in only the most normative of ways. Attempting to prove oneself adult can be a constant and arduous task.

Reason: Intersectional Explorations

So far in this chapter we have theorised around disability as a form of oppression playing out at the border zone of youth, considering the relationships of both 'disability' and 'youth' to 'the unreasonable'. Erevelles (2011) points out, however, that concentrating only on disability fails to acknowledge the relationships between disability and global capitalism, heteropatriarchy, white supremacy and colonialism, and how disability relates to other forms of Otherness under these conditions (see also discussion of ableism in Chapter 6). Our interrogation of 'reasonableness' needs to be similarly intersectional. In a moving introductory chapter, Erevelles (2011) writes of her family's experiences when her husband, Robert, was diagnosed with cancer. At this time Robert began having seizures. Erevelles explains that she and Robert were afraid that if Robert had a seizure in public with nobody that knew him around, his black male disabled body would not be met with care, support or assistance, but threatened with the risk of death. His involuntary movements happening within racist, patriarchal and ableist structures would mark his body as unruly, unreasonable and dangerous to a frightened stranger armed with a gun. If we reflect back on the infantilisation faced by our 51-year-old male wheelchair-using youth-worker trying to access the train with this in mind, we may begin to wonder about the conditions that made his whiteness invisible in this story. Would the story have been different (or told differently) if he was a disabled man of colour? My point here isn't to discredit the particular stories told and analysed thus far, or simply to insert gender/sexuality/class/race into them. Rather, the point I wish to make is that we need to consider what else is going on around the making of un/reasonable bodies at the border zone of youth. We see from Erevelles that to be black is to be deemed dangerously unreasonable.

Furthermore, feminist scholars have pointed out that whilst reason has been prioritised as factual, scientific and masculine, emotion has been considered an oppositional and unreasonable feminine response (Jaggar 1989; Mackenzie and Stoljar 2000; Nagl-Docekal 1999). Gender, therefore, is another important point of consideration in the making of un/reasonable bodies. A story told by Freyja, the directress of the Independent Living Centre in Reykjavik, Iceland, helps us to explore this further. Freyja told the following story to introduce the philosophies of Independent Living (IL) at a conference debating the feasibility of a new law, which would give disabled people the right to hire their own personal assistants:

> You go into a shop and in front of you are two pairs of shoes: some beautiful high-heeled shoes, and some ugly, boring, 'practical' ones. You tell the shop assistant you want the high-heels. You'd be surprised if she turned to you and said, 'are you sure that's a good idea, I don't think they'll be good for your feet, what if you fall? You have to buy the comfortable flat shoes'. You'd tell her that it's up to you which shoes you buy, and you want the high-heels. But these 'it's for your own good attitudes' are the kind disabled people face on a daily basis. IL is about having the freedom to make your own decisions, and make your own mistakes, like everybody else. (My telling of a story told by Freyja in Haraldsdóttir and Ágústsdóttir 2012)

Freyja's presentation was well received. Whereas before Freyja's talk the discussion was icily revolving around the amount of assistance disabled people should be entitled to, Freya's presentation led to laughter and jokes around women's 'need' (and this is how it was expressed by audience members) for high-heeled shoes. The main point Freyja was making in this talk, however, was of course not only to do with high-heeled shoes. The hall was overflowing with politicians of varying levels (including the Icelandic president and the elected mayor), disabled people of varying ages, some of whom were affiliated to and/or representing disabled people's organisations, parents of disabled children, and those employed as PAs and/or other disability 'professionals', along with their union representatives. There was conflict within the room as to whether the new law was 'feasible'. Arguments against feasibility were:

1. It was expensive.

2. Disabled people would take advantage by taking on more assistance than required.

3. Current services did not have time to implement changes.

As in current British politics, a disabled person was seen as 'a fiscal burden but one who deserves the support and succour of the community' (Hughes 2001: 24). The room was full of Mr Reasonables harbouring ableist perspectives that 'in a democracy disabled people should be treated fairly on the basis of toleration. Such a stance does not however suggest that disability is considered a reasonable and an acceptable form of diversity, or indeed that disability can be celebrated' (Campbell 2012: 213). There was acknowledgement that disabled people needed assistance and a place to live. Yet many felt this should be a charitable offering that disabled people should be grateful for, rather than in control of (Barton 1993). Freyja was representing the ILC, advocating for other disabled people and trying to create space for subjugated knowledges within established, hierarchical structures (Code 2000). Freyja's point in this particular story she was telling was that disabled people should be allowed the autonomy to make decisions about their lives (the argument at the crux of the independent living movement – discussed further in Chapter 4). To make disabled people's right to assistance 'common-sense' within the structure she found herself within, Freyja set it within a normative neoliberal consumerist discourse; 'fairness' and 'equality' revolved around women's right to be a consumer of a normatively gendered product.

Let us unpick Freyja's argument further. Although Freyja herself didn't stipulate the right should only be of women (disabled or non-disabled) to buy high-heeled shoes, this was how it was interpreted by the audience. Freyja's argument therefore came to revolve around an assumption that we all share common-sense knowledge that buying high-heeled shoes is what women 'do'. We could go as far as saying that high-heeled shoes symbolise what women 'should be'. As we see in Chapter 6, gendered presumptions and binaries can be oppressive. Freyja's employment of this normatively gendered argument, however, was understood as *reasonable* because it tactically played into the patriarchal power constructed upon gender norms and binaries; reasonable normativity was required by the normative masculinity of the very *reasonable* environment. Furthermore, by strategically 'buying into' stereotyped feminine roles, Freyja was asserting herself as female, a gender identity disabled people are often denied.

Playing into the structures she had on offer to her was then a strategic move for Freyja to make disabled people's right to assistance appear reasonable. Yet, once again (as always) there are missing analyses of the above story. A reading is always partial, and other readings can always be made. It is important to think about what it means that this story was set in Iceland, a relatively wealthy, predominately white country in the global north, with a strong welfare state, low rates of immigration and a small population. Furthermore, although her young disabled female body may be considered unruly and unreasonable, Freyja also occupies more privileged positions. Freyja is white, middle-class and something of a celebrity within the country for her campaigning around disability rights. These positions of privilege help Freyja to be understood as reasonable. If Freyja was trans*, black, poor, or working class this may have been more difficult. Moreover, if she had chosen a less normative anecdote, less easily rendered reasonable within the context she was speaking in, her argument may have been read differently. What is considered un/reasonable is contextual both in terms of the environment we are in, and the ways in which our embodiment is understood. This means certain avenues of resistance which are open to some, are unavailable to others (discussed further in Chapter 6). It also means there are differences in the ways young people are allowed to navigate the border zone of youth.

Short Term Survival vs. Long Term Unsettling Projects

As Kittay and Carlson (2010) point out, to reason is to be considered human (see also Stainton, 2001). With entwined ableism and adultism in mind, it is understandable that in the stories of Freyja, Bjarne and Colin, we see a compulsion to employ arguments based on norms of reason, reasonableness and through this, 'sameness' (disabled young people are no different from everybody else). Furthermore, we see in the next chapter that adulthood, reasonableness, and autonomy are all implicated in one-another; for autonomy to be allowed, one has to be considered a 'reasonable' adult. It is also important to note that the stories of Colin, Bjarne and Freyja all demonstrate resistance as disabled young people and their advocates struggle to resist their societal positionings. Nevertheless, the constant fight for subjectivity through the rhetoric of reason has consequences. For Colin, demonstrating adult reasonableness meant proving himself above and beyond his non-disabled peers, giving him little space to rest. Similarly, Bjarne's mother worried that Bjarne had little space to 'be young' (in whatever form this may take).[1] Finally for Freyja, crossing the border zone of youth into reasonable adulthood, meant (at least periodically) buying into gendered norms that could prove harmful to or unavailable to others (Sothern, 2007). What we lose through an argument based on adulthood normativity and reason, therefore, is the opportunity to become in a multitude of different ways, or indeed 'be' young people (in whatever form this may take). Over the next three chapters I continue to struggle with concepts of subjectivity, autonomy and agency that have been key to disabled people's movements (Greenstein and Graby 2013).

---

1   All of these concerns are discussed further in later chapters. For more on gender and normativity as discussed in relation to Freyja's story see Chapter 6; for more on fights for adulthood independence as discussed in relation to Colin's story see Chapter 4; and for more on 'being young' as discussed in relation to Bjarne's story, see Chapter 5.

Through this chapter we have seen that these are things largely and problematically only granted to people who can prove themselves adult/ reasonable enough. I turn my gaze to think further about the tying of reason with autonomy, through a rhetoric of becoming-independent-adult.

Chapter 4
From Adulthood Independence to Continuing Relational Autonomy

[D]isability touches on [an …] entrenched understanding of what it is to be a subject at all.

(Shildrick 2004)

This chapter is also about disabled people's fights to be considered a subject. In the previous chapter I thought about this in terms of adulthood 'reason'. Philosophers have long argued that to be considered 'reasonable' (as in, able to 'reason'), one must also prove themselves an autonomous being, and this has implications for disabled people, who are often construed as dependent (Kittay and Carlson 2010). In this chapter, therefore, I hone in on the requirement of 'adulthood independence' to think further about disabled people's struggles to be considered an 'I'. Rather than asserting individuality however, my focus will be relational. Throughout the chapter I will think about young people's informal and formal relationships – with parents, families and friends, employers and personal assistants (PAs). My main focus, however, will be on the expectations of these relationships to change through the life course; specifically the shift between so-imagined dependent childhood, and independent adulthood – the middle ground between this being the time we know as 'youth'. Titchkosky (2007) asks us to 'watch our watchings' and 'read our readings'; pointing out that the way we understand 'disability' alters the way we understand our encounters with 'disability' (something, Goodley and Runswick-Cole 2012a, put to work). Stimulated by Titchkosky (2007) and Goodley and Runswick-Cole (2012a), I begin with three (unsatisfactory) readings of the same story which depicts a relational moment between one young disabled person and her mother. After the main body of the chapter – where I learn from disabled people's and feminist movements about the meaning of 'independence' and 'autonomy', I will return to offer a fourth (slightly more satisfactory, but by no means complete) reading. I'll argue that rather than think about youth-as-becoming-independent-adult, we should think about it as a time of dynamic and increasing relations of interdependency, within which autonomy is at times enabled, and at other times denied.

Three Readings (and a 'To Be Continued') of the Same Story

To set the scene, I will introduce you to 16-year-old Meow, a member of the art group, Boom. As detailed in the introductory chapter, whilst I was at Boom members crafted their 'best-ever future world' ideas. Alongside this, however, we chatted about others things: school/college, families, friends and weekend plans. One week, Meow told me of a weekend plan she was particularly excited about: she and her friend were planning to go to a nightclub for under-18s. Although Meow usually got the bus home, that day her Mum came to pick her up. I recorded the delicate incident that followed in my research diary:

> Meow's Mum came in to see her artwork. As they were leaving I shouted bye to Meow, and, remembering about her plans for the weekend added, 'Enjoy your night out'. Meow's Mum turned to look at her, 'we've talked about this ...'. The conversation went on as they left the room. I hope she forgives me!! (Research diary, 9th November 2011, Boom fourth session)

Feeling bad that I'd got Meow into trouble, the following week I apologised and asked Meow if she'd made it to the club. Her response was that she was 'still thinking about it'. Although unsure what she meant, I felt I'd already done my share of damage and didn't press her for more information!

Reading One:
We are Unaware of Meow's Label of Intellectual Impairment

If we were unaware of Meow's label of intellectual impairment, we would probably see this story as typical of the kinds of dialogues 16-year-olds have with their parents; negotiating 'being able to go out, to stay out late, to take part in ordinary teenage experiences' (Murray 2002: 43). Based on normative developmental discourse (Burman 2008), we see Meow and her mother clash as they work out together the murky period between childhood dependency and adulthood independence.

Reading Two:
A Dominant (or Medical/Individual) Approach to
Thinking about Disability

Aware of Meow's label of 'intellectual impairment', however, interpretations perhaps differ. As a disabled person, particularly with a label of 'intellectual impairment', we may consider Meow as 'vulnerable' and 'dependent' and therefore support her mother's decision to not allow her to go out.

We may hold the paternalistic attitude that nightclubs are dangerous and not suitable for disabled people with labels of 'intellectual impairment'.

Reading Three:
A Social Model Approach to Thinking about Disability

Disabled people and disability studies scholars have noted that increased levels of adult surveillance and paternalistic attitudes in the lives disabled young people mean they are not allowed the same freedoms as their non-disabled peers to make their own mistakes (Hughes, Russell and Paterson 2005; Priestley 2003; Veck 2002). With this view in mind, we would probably be vigilant to barriers that prevent Meow from taking part in the same activities as her peers. We may, in fact, view Meow's Mum as one of these barriers: overprotectively preventing Meow from having the freedom she craves, denying her access to 'youthful' spaces and hindering her striving for adulthood independence (Goodley and Runswick-Cole 2012a). Some may even goes as far as viewing Meow's mother as an agent of mundane disablism (Thomas 1999), contributing to her, and other disabled people's positionings as 'eternal children' (Baron, Riddell and Wilson 1999).

Reading Four:
To Be Continued ...

I will argue through this chapter, however, that none of the above analyses are satisfactory. Each rests upon a normatively imagined and idealised figure of an insufficiently contextualised, reasonable, independent and masculinised adult subject, who acts in *his* own interest, and autonomously from those around *him* (Mackenzie and Stoljar 2000a). The aim of this chapter is to contextualise the relationship between both people in this scenario; to think about relationships as multi-directional (Walmsley 1993); and to consider how relationships can both enable and deny autonomy (Mackenzie and Stoljar 2000a). I am thankful to Graby and Greenstein (2013) in this discussion, whose paper I have continually referred back to whilst (re)writing this chapter. Following these scholars and activists, although wary of Western conceptualisations of 'independence' as being about 'doing things on your own', I introduce disabled people's (re)conceptualisations of 'independence' alongside feminist concepts of 'relational autonomy' (Mackenzie and Stoljar 2000b). Only after these musings, will I be able to offer you a fourth reading of Meow and her mother's relational story.

Rethinking Independence One:
Lessons from the Icelandic Independent Living Centre

Independent: *adjective*
free from outside control; not subject to another's authority
not depending on another for livelihood or subsistence
capable of thinking or acting for oneself
not connected with another or with each other; separate.

(Oxford Online Dictionary 2013)

The above dictionary definition relays the implicit idea that 'independence' is about 'doing things on your own'; a depiction that can prove harmful to the often connected lives of disabled people (Ware 2005). Freyja and Embla, along with their colleagues at the independent living centre in Reykjavik (NPA Miðstöðin 2013), were engaged in daily battles which involved asserting disabled people's independence. Yet, they had different ideas as to what 'independence' meant. The independent living centre Freyja and Embla work at is a user-controlled cooperative for personal assistance which was established by Freyja in 2010. In a recent publication, *Free*, the centre is described as such:

> The cooperative is based on the principles of the Independent Living philosophy and the European Network of Independent Living (ENIL) requirements for membership. The purpose of the centre is to assist disabled people in recruiting and organizing personal assistance through peer support and take responsibility for all the administrative work. Also it is to offer training to personal assistants, the public and the government about the Independent Living philosophy and participate actively in international collaboration concerning Independent Living. (Haraldsdóttir and Sigurðardttir 2011: 37)

Terms such as 'cooperative' and 'network' jar with the individualistic dictionary definition of 'independent' above. As the managing director, Freyja was the only full-time member of staff and paid employee at the independent living centre. Embla works voluntarily part-time, as the chairwoman. Many of Freyja and Embla's daily battles involve asserting that they and other independent living centre members have the right to 'independence' through the use of assistance and support. Independence, those within disability movements have long argued, is about something other than 'doing things for yourself' (Hughes 2001). On its website, the *European Network on Independent Living* (ENIL) writes of the importance of defining 'independent living' in order 'to challenge the misleading applications of the English use of [independence]' (ENIL 1992). They write:

> We believe fundamentally that all individuals have the right to live independently in the community regardless of their disability. But it is important to note the sense in which we use the word 'independence', because it is crucial to everything we are saying. We do not use the term 'independent' to mean someone who can do everything for themselves, but to indicate someone who has taken control of their life and is choosing how that life is led. (Brisenden 1986: 178)

According to Brisenden (1986), for those involved in the independent living movement, 'independence' is about being allowed the opportunity to make choices about what happens in one's own life; something disabled people continue to be denied. In 1989 he further wrote that '[i]ndependence is not linked to the physical or intellectual capacity to care for oneself without assistance; independence is created by having assistance when and how one requires it' (cited in Bracking and Cowan 1998). The independent living movement functions, therefore, to enable disabled people to have control over their own assistance, so they can choose how their life is led.

Like the pioneering activists in the 1960s and 1970s (see Evans 2003; Zukas 1975), Freyja, Embla and others at the independent living centre, had their own definitions of what it meant to lead an 'independent' life. In their recently published book entitled *Free*, Freyja tells us that to her IL 'means being able to make my own decisions, create my own lifestyle so I can be fully myself' (Freyja cited in Haraldsdóttir and Sigurdardttir 2011: 28). Others tell us more about the meaning of IL:

Embla: 'To me independent living means being able to be a woman'. (7)

Ragnar (four-years-old): 'To me independent living means being able to live at home with my mom, dad and siblings as well as going to a playschool like most 4-year-old boys do'. (8)

Áslaug (tenth grade at school): 'To me independent living means being able to control how to shape my own life'. (11)

Gísli (26-year-old man): 'To me independent living is being able to study at the University of Iceland and to work as an organist in Sunday school at my church'. (12)

Ásdís (sign language professional and poet): 'To me independent living means being able to have my own family and a dog'. (15)

Karl (25-year-old artist and security guard): 'To me independent living means being able to live on my own and do what I want, when I want'. (16)

Hallgrímur (33-year-old computer specialist): 'To me independent living is the key to being able to live a free life on my own terms'. (19)

Bjarney (10-years-old): 'To me independent living means being able to play in my leisure time the way I want to'. (20)

Jón (38-year-old swimming coach): 'To me independent living means having the opportunity to live life to the fullest'. (23)

Snædís (second grade college student): 'To me independent living is a dream that must come true'. (24)

Finnbogi (10-years-old): 'To me independent living means being able to choose to play Shrek on costume day at my school'. (27)

(Haraldsdóttir and Sigurðardttir 2011)

For those at the independent living centre, those involved in the independent living movement, and other disabled activists, 'independence' has much more holistic meanings than the *Online Oxford Dictionary* made out; having little to do with being alone. Although conceptions of independent living such as 'being able to live on my own and do what I want, when I want' (Karl in Haraldsdóttir and Sigurðardttir 2011: 16) err towards conventional conceptions of independence, for others it had different meanings: being able to play Shrek on costume day or to live life as a woman (I consider Embla's assertion that IL enables her to be a woman further in Chapter 6). In the last chapter we saw 'humanness' being related to the capacity for 'reason' and 'autonomy' (Kittay and Carlson 2010). In their study of people with labels of intellectual impairment, however, Bogdan and Taylor (1998) found personhood to be formed through relationships. It seems those at the independent living centre conceptualised independence as something similarly connected: 'being able to live at home with my Mom, Dad and siblings as well as going to playschool' (Haraldsdóttir and Sigurðardttir 2011: 8), or 'being able to have my own family and a dog' (Haraldsdóttir and Sigurðardttir 2011: 15).

Rethinking Independence Two: Feminist Lessons of Relational Autonomy

This connected notion of 'independence' is similar to feminist ideas of relational autonomy (Greenstein and Graby 2013). Just as some within disability studies have controversially rejected the term 'independence' (see, for example, B. Gibson 2006; Shildrick 2009), some Feminists have rejected the term 'autonomy', deeming it 'inherently masculinist' (Mackenzie and Stoljar 2000a: 3). For these Feminists, autonomy is a problematic concept 'exemplified by the self-sufficient, rugged male individualist, rational maximizing chooser of libertarian theory' (Mackenzie and Stoljar 2000a: 5); our Mr Reasonable, perhaps. We challenged the individualism inherent to ideas of libertarian theory in Chapter 1, and also the notion of 'reason' most fully in the previous chapter. With this in mind perhaps such a rejection of the term 'autonomy' is not surprising. Code (2000) suggests, however, that we should not be too quick to reject autonomy. As a concept both pedestalled and denied to many, it is unsurprising *and* legitimate that those oppressed through the denial of autonomy, such as disabled people, strive towards it. Similarly Graby and Greenstein (2013) argue that rejecting the term 'independence' means going against the principles of disabled people's movements and risks neglecting vital conversations about autonomy and consent within relationships.

Furthermore, when we think some more about the meanings and uses of the term 'autonomy', it becomes particularly pertinent to disabled people. Although its precise meaning is disputed, autonomy is used in numerous debates including those around freedom of speech, euthanasia, reproductive technologies (Mackenzie and Stoljar 2000a); all topics very relevant to disabled people's lives (Tilley, Walmsley, Earle and Atkinson 2012; Tremain 2006). Taking the views of disabled people discussed above into account, then, we see that autonomy, like 'independence', can be used to mean having control over, and choosing how to lead one's life (Brisenden 1986; Greenstein and Graby 2013). Importantly, we also come to realise that these choices are, for all of us (not just disabled people), always only made with, alongside and dependent upon others. Morris points this out:

> [...] we all depend on water coming out of the tap when we turn it on, while a disabled person [...] depends on someone to help her get dressed in the morning. However, when non-disabled people talk about water coming out of the tap, the issue is whether the water company is reliable; when they talk about [disabled person] being dependent on an assistant, the issue for them is what they see as her helplessness created by her physical limitations. (Morris 1991: 137–8)

Power in Relationships

Although writers come at relational autonomy from varying perspectives, at the core is a shared conviction that *all* people are socially embedded; autonomy can therefore only ever happen within relationships (Mackenzie and Stoljar 2000a). Furthermore, the forms these relationships are allowed to take are mediated by race, class, gender, ethnicity, dis/ability, sexuality, geographical location and so on, as there are differing social norms and expectations relating to these positionings (Mackenzie and Stoljar 2000a). Autonomy, therefore, isn't something that resides within bodies and minds, but is socially and culturally co-constituted meaning different relations can impede or enhance an agent's capacity for autonomy (Kittay 1999; Mackenzie and Stoljar 2000b). We see the potential for autonomy to be granted or denied in another story from Freyja:

> I had an interview to work with children at a nursery. As soon as I entered the room [with my assistant] I saw how surprised the interviewer was. She didn't even try to hide it. The first thing she said was, 'so I see you're disabled … what would *you* do here?' 'Well, I'd do what the job specification requires of me: I'd look after the children'. 'But how?' the interviewer asked. She just couldn't get her head around a woman with a physical impairment working with children. I'd worked in a nursery before, it wasn't that difficult to understand: my assistants did the physical stuff I couldn't, while I did the more emotional side of it. To kids, it just isn't a problem. (My version of Freyja's story, research diary, 16th February 2011)

As a disabled person Freyja challenges normative assumptions of whole, independent bodies that carry out a job on their own (Goodley and Roets 2008). 'So I see you're disabled', is an accusation: why did *you* bother to apply for this job? Yet, as Freyja points out, Freyja and her assistant together spending time with children has the potential to be both overtly relational *and* constitutive of autonomy. One result of Freyja first being given the right to assistance, and then allowed to work within this relationship, is that Freyja and her assistant would both be waged (Freyja by the nursery, and the assistant through funding of the independent living centre) and therefore (problematically) considered 'productive' within (neo)liberal economies (see Chapter 1). Wages and production are both requirements of the 'adult' citizen. Therefore, a wage could allow Freyja some access into the world of 'adulthood'. Furthermore, a wage would allow both people involved in this relationship to separately make choices which those without finance are not allowed. However, the story also alerts us to the potential for this autonomy to be denied. As the interviewer's Western, individualistic conceptualisation of 'independence' clashes with the connectivity of Freyja's life she fails to see the productive potential of the network that can be established. This means she maintains traditional and oppressive assumptions of disabled people as unproductive, and indeed, childlike. Thinking back to the last chapter, as a disabled person Freyja is deemed *unreasonable* in her dependency.

To fight against their positioning as unreasonably dependent, independent living movements have argued that traditional conceptualisations of 'caring' wrongly position disabled people as helpless and burdensome. They have therefore repositioned carer-disabled person relationships by rejecting notions of 'care' in favour of 'assistance' (Hughes, McKie, Hopkins and Watson 2005; Morris 1997).

Thus, whereas traditionally the relationship of 'carer-cared for' is one where the carer holds the power, independent living movements realign this to 'employed-employer', where the disabled person is in control (Hughes, McKie et al. 2005; McLaughlin 2006; Morris 1997). For Morris (1997) the reason for this is clear: the types of 'care' disabled people have traditionally been subject to amount to forms of oppression which have left them powerless, in the control of others, and open to abuse. It is important to note that this is not only a historical argument. In 2011 a BBC Panorama documentary (Kenyon 2011) revealed the systemic and shocking levels of abuse people with labels of intellectual impairment were subject to in so-called 'care' homes, such as *Winterbourne View* in the UK (Cave 2013).

Some within disability studies, however, have argued that independent living movements have not gone far enough in challenging individualistic and hierarchical, money-based economies (Hughes, McKie et al. 2005). Kittay and Carlson (2010) point out that those most in danger of being deemed 'unreasonable', are those with the most 'profound' impairments. For Kittay (1999), therefore, it is with these people that any conversations around 'justice' and 'equality' should begin, as their autonomy is most readily denied. Yet, it has been noted that these same people have been left aside in independent living movements (Ferguson and Ferguson 2001). This is particularly pertinent in the case of Winterbourne and other forms of institutional abuse.

Askheim (2003) points out that in independent living movements 'the [disabled person] is seen as an autonomous individual and the relationship between the receiver of services and the care worker is regarded as that found in ordinary employment, where the care worker executes the user's "orders"' (2003: 328). One worry to emerge from this is that people with intellectual impairments may not be in positions to implement the level of user control required as an employer. Therefore, in order to incorporate people with intellectual impairments into the movement, the principle of user control may potentially be compromised (Askheim 2003). As there are arguably greater power differentials between people with intellectual impairments and their often non-disabled assistants, the disabled person's relative power can potentially be more easily undermined.

The possibility of this problematic power dynamic occurring was illustrated to me during an encounter with 26-year-old Arnar. Arnar is a board member of the independent living centre in Reykjavik with a label of intellectual impairment and strong views on independence. He gave a presentation about his independent life with the support of his assistant:

Arnar stands by the microphone, next to his assistant. The *PowerPoint* behind him shows pictures from his life. Arnar's name is on the programme: it is *his* presentation about *him* being an independent man, yet his assistant does much of the 'talking'. Occasionally she turns to him for clarification, at which point he leans in to the microphone, and shouts a defiant 'já' (yes) or 'ekki' (no). He (through his assistant) explains that he used to live in a residential home. 'Did you like it there?' his assistant asks him, 'ekki!' Arnar is sure he prefers his life today, living in his own place and hiring his own assistants which enable him to live independently. He tells us about this life where, with assistance, he does his shopping, cooks his meals, goes to work, and so on. (Research diary, 14th March 2012)

Despite what others may see as his dependencies on his assistants, Arnar considers his life one of independence. He demonstrates this through his presentation which, at first, fits into indepent living philosophies as he uses his assistant to demonstrate his relational autonomy. Yet, later I record the following:

A member of the audience asks Arnar a question: 'Do you have any brothers?' Arnar replies, yes, he does. The assistant seems hesitant, but leans towards the microphone, 'No, he doesn't'. Although non-disabled, as the mother of a disabled son, Arnar's assistant is a board member of the independent living centre and good friends with the rest of the board, who are sitting beside me. She looks guiltily at them before saying: 'I shouldn't have said that, I just broke the first rule of assistance'. (Research diary, 14th March 2012)

Believing that Arnar does not have a brother, Arnar's assistant steps in to correct Arnar, and thus restricts the story he has to tell. Arnar did not speak back to his assistant, and the conference moved on, I speculate, with no long-term negative effect on Arnar's life (and it is important to stress that this is only one moment from Arnar's life). Yet, the concerns are a) that Arnar's assistant has placed a question mark over the authenticity of his statements, with possible future implications; and b) that the scenario could happen in situations with greater impact.

The same afternoon that Arnar presented, there was also a presentation by a representative from a Swedish independent living centre called JAG, whose members all have 'multiple, severe disabilities including some kind of intellectual disability' (Tengström n.d.). In Swedish, the initials JAG stand for Equality, Assistance and Inclusion, and the word 'JAG' itself means 'I'. As the speaker from JAG went on, she described what 'I' means to JAG members: 'not we, not me, but I. Not *we* are doing this together; not *he* is doing this *with me*; but *I* am doing this with assistance'. JAG believes that every person can demonstrate self-determination; it is a matter of understanding particular forms of communication. 'Self-determination can [...] be regarded as an act of interdependence, where one individual works with others to derive and meet goals, and be autonomous, active members of their community' (Kelm 2009: 118). The JAG model works through a layering system. The disabled person has a 'legal proxy', somebody who knows them well, can support their right to 'self-determination' and understands their methods of communication.

Although, as I discussed earlier, parents have sometimes been seen a barrier to young disabled people's independence (McLaughlin 2006; Ryan and Runswick-Cole 2008), JAG members are routinely represented by their parents (Askheim 2003). Parents are seen as potential routes rather than barriers to independence for disabled people (Ryan and Runswick-Cole 2008).

The next layer is the 'service guarantor' who directly supervises and manages the day-to-day activities of the assistants:

> The service guarantor is a person who knows the user well and who has the task to secure that the user has the control over the arrangement. A part of it is the responsibility to teach the assistants how to interpret the user's signals of communication. In the first period after the assistants have been employed the service guarantor therefore works together with them until the assistants have got to know the user. (Askheim 2003: 336)

Finally there are the assistants themselves. JAG continue to work around this term which asserts individual subjectivity, yet, these 'layers' make the 'I' of JAG profoundly connected.

If we look at historical and continuing institutionalisation we see why defining yourself as an individual subject (an 'I') could be so important to disabled people, particularly those with labels of intellectual impairment. Overboe (2007) reminds us of the continuing presence of a subhuman label in disabled people's lives, and in Chapter 6 I consider the importance of subjectivity in relation to gender and sexuality. We see that disabled young people are not only threatened with institutionalisation, but disabled people's devalued status reinforces a continued eugenic drive which threatens young disabled women (Hall 2011; Roets, Adams and Hove 2006; Tilley et al. 2012). My point here isn't particularly of interrogating or critiquing independent living movements. Rather, I am trying to learn lessons from disabled people about what it may mean to think about 'personhood' outside of the ableism that is inherent to discourses of 'adulthood' (Chapter 2). As this adulthood is reliant upon 'independence' (Lahelma and Gordon 2008), this includes interrogating what is meant by 'independence'. Importantly for me asserting their subjectivity was something young disabled people I spent time with were continually struggling for.

Relational Autonomy and Interdependency

So far, I have used both disabled people's and feminist critiques of 'autonomy' and 'independence'. However, carer/cared-for dualities have led to some conflict between feminist and disabled people's discussions of care and assistance (Kröger 2009; McLaughlin 2006). In order to assert their own autonomy, some feminists have highlighted the devalued gendered connotations of caring, considered the natural role of women in both paid and unpaid situations (Kröger 2009). Yet disability rights advocates have highlighted that these discussions fail to examine the role of the recipient of care, therefore passively maintaining the oppressive locations of disabled people (McLaughlin 2006). Furthermore, independent living movements have at times been guilty of devaluing the 'caring work', which is largely performed by women – many of whom are women of colour (Hughes, McKie et al. 2005; Kittay 1999). Thus, feminist and disabled people's movements have sometimes been seen as separate and oppositional to one-another (Hughes, McKie et al. 2005). For Hughes et al. (2005), however, such a duality is the result of fighting battles based upon the norms of those already in power. Rather than see feminist arguments which focus on valuing the carer, and disabled people's arguments of valuing the cared for as oppositional, Hughes et al. (2005: 269) ask us to 'try to think past or beyond a world in which women and disabled people are constituted as the "negative of positive", as inferior or defective men' (a sentence which perhaps sums up the ethos of this book). This means not always thinking individually, but relationally without losing autonomy and subjectivity within these relationships. Both Hughes et al. (2005) and Kittay (1999) highlight that often all within the caring–cared-for relationship are marginalised. Rather than thinking about carers and cared-for, as distinct groups with distinct agendas, Kittay considers how dis/ability and in/dependence intersect with gender, race and poverty. In doing this she points out that:

> Care of dependents – dependency work – is most commonly assigned to those in a society with the least status and power. Furthermore, attention to diversity cautions us not to assume that this is still another universal attribute of women, for not all women care for dependents. Caring labor is assigned to women differently depending on race, class, ability and age, and men of marginalized groups are often also assigned to care for dependents. (Kittay 1999: 16)

Thus Kittay (1999) urges the importance of caring for *all* within such relationships. This means beginning, not with an assumption of independence, but with an assumption of dependence. For Kittay (1999), when we appreciate that the carer is also the cared for; the common struggle becomes one not of fighting for individual rights, but ensuring each is cared for, by allowing for autonomy within relationships. For Graby and Greenstein (2013), this means seeing autonomy not as a destination, or something any of us can 'have', but as a continual struggle that we learn to do with others. Walmsley's (1993) research around the caring roles of women with intellectual impairment makes a similar point:

> Examples of the views and experiences of women with learning difficulties show that caring and dependency, far from being dichotomous, are on a continuum. We are all dependent to a greater or lesser degree on others. And so-called dependents can themselves be carers. (Walmsley 1993: 136)

We are urged to appreciate that 'who is the carer is in the eye of the beholder' (Walmsley 1993: 136). 'Expand[ing] our definition of caring to encompass not just physical tasks but also the emotional' (Morris 1991: 167). For this 'youth' and 'disability' project, considering the interdependent, multidirectional nature of caring relationships, can help us to a) question why young people breaking away from their parents has come to be seen as such a 'natural' Western phenomenon; and b) rethink child/parent relationships in ways which are more inclusive to the lived-experiences of young disabled people.

Importantly, reconsidering relationships in this way also seems to better reflect the lived-realities of young disabled people's lives. Murray (2002: 43) reports that when asked about their relationships with their parents, young disabled people in her study 'agree[d] that their parents sometimes worried about them too much, [but] understood why this was the case. They thought it was reasonable for their parents to worry (all of them had had very unpleasant experiences), but were keen to work out ways of being able to go out, to stay out late, to take part in ordinary teenage experiences'. Colin and Gabby from the Youth Forum (introduced more fully in Chapter 3) felt similarly. Talking about their parents, they said:

> **Colin:** 'Just because you're disabled they don't let you make your own mistakes. I've got a sister who's non-disabled and she can do what she wants, when she wants and my mum's okay with that. I try doing the same and I'm not allowed!'

> **Gabby:** 'They might treat us different because we're in a wheelchair. They might think we're vulnerable to accidents and things'.

> **Colin:** 'It's the way your parents are brought up. They're brought up with the medical model and they don't really know the social model and because of that they're scared to let go'.

> (First Futures workshop with YF, 23rd November 2011)

Although they acknowledged that most young people battled with their parents, Colin and Gabby thought that as disabled young people their situation was harder. Yet, although they found their parents' protectiveness frustrating, they didn't consider this a fault of their parents. Rather, it was due to their parents not knowing alternative discourses of disability. It was a matter of giving their parents access to different ways of thinking about disability (which, of course, is not always an easy task).

To this end, most of the young disabled people I spoke to looked forward to a time when they would be able to have more control over their social lives. Sometimes, particularly at YF, disabled young people wished their parents allowed them the same freedoms as their non-disabled siblings. Many envisioned their lives becoming more separate from their parents as they grew older. Yet, there didn't seem to be a desire to escape 'parental constraint'. In Boom, feelings were, in fact, to the contrary. In the first couple of sessions with the group, I asked Boom members to imagine they were time-travelling reporters, travelling to their best ever future worlds, and filling in 'Reports from the Future' to bring back to the present day. One of the questions asked the young people how they would fit into the Best Ever Future World. For Meow, this was a difficult question as she couldn't decide on the ideal living situation. She flitted between living with her family or with her friends. In an interview she told me she may want to move from her Mum's house when she was 'about 30'. Eventually she decided the best situation was to have two big houses next door to each other, one for her family and another for her friends. She could switch between the two. This was reflected in a piece of artwork Meow called *My Life in the Future*. In it she drew a 'rainbow castle' for Meow's family to live in, next door to a more (to put it in Meow's words) 'ordinary castle' for her friends.

Meow does not want to be restricted to *only* spending time with her family. Yet neither does she see her parents as constricting her future adulthood endeavours, or a hindrance to time she may choose to spend with her friends. Goodley and Runswick-Cole's (2013) findings are similar. In relation to a project considering disabled people's resilience through the life course, they report that 'while families offer support and alliance these same families share experiences of disablism. Inevitably, as young people grow older then the locus of support expands to include friends' (Goodley and Runswick-Cole 2012b: 82). Listening and considering the lives of young disabled people through this chapter leads me further to dismiss the common (mis)conception that youth is about becoming-independent. Rather, it is about dynamic and increasing numbers of interdependencies.

Re-reading Meow's Story: A Tale of Struggles of Autonomy within Dynamic and Interdependent Relationships

With our new understandings of independence and relational autonomy in mind, then, I want to come back to think some more about Meow's story that opened the chapter. I left Meow's story posing three possible ways of interpreting this particular scenario between Meow and her mother. Firstly, I suggested that we could see this as a 'normal part of growing up' as Meow strives to move between childhood dependence, and adulthood independence. Yet, it is arguably this assumption, based upon normative developmental discourse that has led to the positioning of disabled people as eternal children. I am therefore resistant to it. Secondly, I pointed out that some may think that nightclubs are not a place for Meow; that, as a young woman with a label of intellectual impairment, she is too 'vulnerable' to go on this night out. Feminist and disability scholars, however, have pointed out that discourses of vulnerability work only to individualise, rather than highlight systemic cultures of violence and rape; taking the blame away from violent systems and perpetrators, and instead placing it upon individuals (Friedman and Valenti 2008; Goodley 2011). Such a reading, therefore, restricts Meow's right to autonomy. Finally, I highlighted that some disability studies scholars have argued that parents can add to the mundane disablism in the lives of their disabled children by themselves restricting their children's independence. Without denying the possibility of this, neither is this an argument I find particularly helpful. It is this latter reading I want to concentrate on now.

Veck (2002) makes this argument in relation to Ray, a mature student with the label of intellectual impairment who is in the process of leaving a 'special unit' at a further education college which he has attended for a number of years. According to Veck:

> Ray often expressed frustration about his relationship with his mother. 'The thing', he [Ray] asserted, 'is that she doesn't get it, that I'm a man'. When asked what he meant by this Ray was non-responsive, but he clearly felt that his mother did not consider him to be an adult who was capable of living independently. (Veck 2002: 534)

Veck (2002) goes on to metaphorically conceptualise Ray's life as trapped in a 'parent–child' discourse, sustained as 'staff [at college], officials and Ray's mother act as a "net-like organisation" that fixed "a normative gaze" upon Ray' (532). I do not know Ray or his relationship with his mother, and do not wish to completely discredit this *particular* story. Yet, I nevertheless have a problem with this interpretation. If we are thinking about autonomy as relational, we need to consider and contextualise all within this relationship: carer/cared for or assistant/assisted relationships 'can have enabling or disabling effects for both' (B.E. Gibson, Brooks, DeMatteo and King 2009: 317). My first problem with Veck's (2002) interpretation of Ray's story is therefore that there is a lack of acknowledgment to the disablist world that Ray's mother is inhabiting along with Ray (Ryan and Runswick-Cole 2008).

Moreover, however, we also see how such individualising practices based upon one particular example, lead to unhelpful assumptions about constituted groups. Ryan and Runswick-Cole (2008) note that 'the actions of mothers have been interpreted as constraints within their [disabled] children's lives, limiting their opportunities and aspirations' (Ryan and Runswick-Cole 2008: 200), and we see this happening here. Veck uses the mother–disabled child relationship in a way which demonises *all* mothers (and the gendering is important to note) of *all* disabled children. The relationship of mother, and disabled offspring, is used as a metaphor to negatively conceptualise the normative gaze surrounding Ray. Let us then reread Meow's story otherwise.

Firstly, we should not deny the unique (prestructured) experiences of Meow's family, which are no doubt influenced by dis/ableist structures and attitudes (Ryan and Runswick-Cole 2008). Colin and Gabby from the YF told us that their parents were more protective of them than their non-disabled siblings. Taking heed of this and other studies (Baron et al. 1999; Horgan 2003; Murray 2002; Priestley 2003), we can speculate that Meow's Mum *is* likely to be more protective of Meow, due to her label of intellectual impairment. However, we should also listen to Murray's (2002) participants who told us that although their parents (like all parents) could sometimes be frustrating, they felt their parents' worries were justified. Growing-up disabled in a dis/ablist world can be both difficult and dangerous (Goodley 2011). Furthermore, we need to consider how, through youth, such networks can grow. Thinking about autonomy as a struggle that happens with others, we can see that there is negotiation between Meow and her Mum. However, this is not necessarily to do with Meow 'breaking away' or becoming-independent, but increasing and dynamic networks of interdependency. To maintain autonomy and subjectivity within these relationships, we have seen, is difficult. Yet the importance of this struggle is something disabled people have taught us through this chapter, which needs to be recognised and fought for.

Conclusion

Of course, reading four is just another reading. The aim of this chapter, however, has been to critically consider the often implicit notion of youth as becoming-independent-adult, and offer an alternative, more inclusive reading of what it could mean to see interdependence as part of the continued becoming of life. Hughes (2001) highlights that critiquing notions of independence has been at the crux of disability activism; we have seen this above. Although 'independence' is part of the dialogue of independent living movements, it seems that for those involved it represents something different to what has become its common-sense usage. Following Graby and

Greenstein (2013), my argument in this chapter has been that disabled people's conceptions of independence are not about 'doing things on your own', and are in fact closer to feminist notions of relational autonomy (Mackenzie and Stoljar 2000b). Under a (neo)liberal agenda, autonomy has been fetishised into something biologically inherent; something you either do or do not have. For disabled youth, this is dangerous. Taking the ideas of relational autonomy and interdependency forward as our theoretical framework, we can begin to understand 'youth' differently. Murray (2002: 21) reported that for her young disabled participants independence was about having the chance to build relationships, and participate in activities alongside peers. Requiring support was not a negative aspect of this, 'on the contrary, the presence of appropriate support allowed for new adventures to take place'. For Freyja, 'independent living means being able to make my own decisions, create my own lifestyle so I can be fully myself' (Freyja cited in Haraldsdóttir and Sigurðardttir 2011: 28). To allow each to be fully oneself is to allow for becoming in a multiplicity of ways. Youth as becoming is about expanding, dynamic and interconnected networks of interdependence. These allow for new experiences as part of a continual becoming of life.

This is not to say, however, that we can afford to become complacent; we must keep at the forefront of our minds the possibility of abuse within relationships. I think about this further in the Chapter 6 where we think about the impact of dependence/independence dualities on young disabled women, with a focus on gender and sexuality. Here autonomy and consent are particularly important (Friedman and Valenti 2008; Greenstein and Graby 2013). For now, however, I follow Graby and Greenstein (2013) in seeing autonomy not as a destination, or something any of us can 'have', but as a continual struggle, and something we learn to do with others. Youth is one stage of life where this struggle continues to shift and be (re)learnt.

The next chapter continue to think about struggles at the border zone of youth through critical engagement with access, space and youth culture.

Chapter 5
Negotiating Space and Constituting 'Problems': Access at the Border Zone of Youth

You can't go clubbing or 'hang out' with your Mum and Dad. Youth culture depends on freedom from adult control but disabled kids – particularly girls – just don't get it (Thomas, 1998).

(Hughes, Russell and Paterson 2005: 9)

Above, Hughes et al. (2005) convey a dominant account of youth culture as risk. A space, perhaps, that allows for the 'unreasonable' non-normativity of youth (Slater f.c.-a), and therefore a space of which young people would prefer their parents to be unaware. Despite the commonly reiterated battles between teenagers and their parents over 'youthful' endeavours, the story goes that youth culture is important to young people's identity formation (Rattansi and Phoenix 2005); 'teenage rebellion' is hailed as an 'identity forming' rite of passage for young people to cross the border zone between child and adult. We touched upon some of the ableism within such assertions in the previous chapter. I discussed how youth functions in relation to a discourse of 'unreasonableness'. We saw that for some young disabled people, such as Colin from the disabled people's organisation's Youth Forum (YF), and Bjarne from Iceland, embracing the unreasonable non-normativity of youth didn't feel like an option on offer. The fight for them was to safely pass across the border zone of youth and reach adulthood. Linger in youth too long, and they were at risk of being rooted in infantilising and childlike discourse.

Yet other young people *did* speak of their identities as young people and/or their desires to access activities and spaces on a par with their non-disabled peers. Meow from art group, Boom, for example, spoke openly about her desire to be considered part of what we may normatively conceive to be 'youth culture'. Fieldwork with Boom started shortly after the beginning of a new academic year. For 16-year-old Meow, that September meant moving from her previously segregated school to study ICT at a mainstream college. She was enjoying the additional freedom that this allowed her: travelling to and from college (and Boom) by bus; lying-in when she had a late start; and finding college staff had more relaxed attitudes than those at her previous school. Like the rest of the group, I asked Meow to begin by filling in the 'Report from the Future' booklets. These introduced the research and provided a place for participants to plan their ideas for their final best ever future world art piece. The second question in the booklet asked Meow the age of her time-travelling avatar. I stressed that this did not have to reflect young people's real age. Meow chose 21. Interviewing Meow later, it seemed 21 represented a time when she would spend more time in places she considers for young people:

Jenny: 'How old's your time traveller?'

Meow: '21'.

Jenny: 'Any reason you went for 21?'

Meow: 'It's just a good age. I'd like to be 21'.

Jenny: 'How come?'

Meow: 'Because you're still young but you have more freedom'.

Jenny: 'What would you do if you had more freedom when you were 21 that you can't do now?'

Meow: 'I'd have more money and I'd go to nightclubs. [Meow turns, attempting to catch the eye of one of the older staff members, and raises her voice] … because they're not for old people'.

(Interview with Meow, 12th October 2012)

Meow wants both the finances and freedom to go clubbing. Furthermore, as nightclubs are spaces she deems 'not for old people' it seems Hughes et al. (2005: 9) and Meow are in agreement: 'You can't go clubbing or "hang out" with your Mum and Dad'. Although I would dispute such assertion for too readily resting on developmental norms (see previous chapter), we see Meow here asserting herself *as* a young person (different to 'old people'). I use this chapter, therefore, to further consider young disabled people's negotiations at the border zone of youth. Without denying the variety of ways young disabled people may access 'youth cultural spaces' (online or offline, for example), the different forms these (sub)cultures may take and the different degrees to which ableism functions within them, I focus on two problems brought to my attention during fieldwork: 1) the in/accessibility of space; and 2) the oppositional discursive positioning sometimes made between disability (particularly certain impairments, such as intellectual impairments) and 'youth culture'. The argument I make is that these problems of space and discourse are intertwined with one-another, and indeed our perceptions of what youth culture is and should be. Finally, complicating the meaning we attribute to 'youth culture' I turn to explore what I deem to be young disabled people's youth cultural negotiations at the border zone of youth.

Before I continue, it is important to point out that although I engage, to an extent, with youth subcultural studies in this chapter, it doesn't pretend to be a literature review which spans recent youth/sub/cultural work and map its (lack of) engagement with disability. There is much interesting and important work to be done here about young disabled people's access to spaces we may deem subcultural, especially in the light of new technologies. Nevertheless, such a conversation is outside the scope of this book. Rather, I use this chapter to utilise some classic subcultural texts which help me to theorise some of the *particular* negotiations of the young people I spent time with, and think about how these (problematically) may or may not be perceived as part of youth culture. I begin by turning now to the young people part of the disabled people's campaigning organisation's Youth Forum (YF), to address the first problem: that of access and space.

A Problem of Inaccessible Space

During the first workshop with YF, I asked the young people to write down things that had annoyed them recently. We placed these in a dustbin, before picking each annoyance out individually and discussing as a group how this may be different in our best ever future world. A group conversation during this went as follows:

> **Jenny**: 'Here it says that you're annoyed about the government taking away places for young people to go. What would be different in our future world?'
>
> **Matthew**: 'Government giving more people more places to go'.
>
> **Margery [youth worker]**: 'What about young disabled people? Does that include us as well?'
>
> **Nathan**: 'Yeah, it includes all of us. Us as well'.
>
> **Mohammed**: 'They need to be accessible'.
>
> **Matthew**: 'Yeah, accessible!'

> (Transcript from first futures workshop with YF, 23rd November 2011)

YF members were frustrated about the diminishing number of places for young people, disabled and non-disabled, to spend time. They argued, however, that as young disabled people their options are fewer than their non-disabled peers, as some spaces are inaccessible to them. Priestley (2003) notes that physical barriers prevent disabled youth from accessing the same arenas as their non-disabled peers. These concerns do not only relate to formal, often government-funded services, but perhaps *especially* to casual, informal settings that young people may choose to spend time (Hughes et al. 2005) such as fast food outlets (Watson et al. 1999), restaurants and pubs (Hirst and Baldwin 1994).

That inaccessible space was a problem for some at YF also became apparent a cameras workshop I ran with the group. Here I asked young people to take pictures as we moved around a city centre. I deliberately left the instructions for young people vague, not mentioning 'disability', as I did not want to assume 'disability' would be the main thing on young people's agendas. Yet, the pictures that came back reflected the disabling inaccessibility of space. Pictures included a large silver step in front of a fast food outlet; Colin, a wheelchair user, trying to negotiate a narrow shop entrance; and then later Colin posing, frustrated as steps are blocking his access to a pub. These pictures support Hughes et al.'s (2005: 11) assertion that 'young disabled people, particularly those with learning difficulties or severe physical impairments will have little experience of the spontaneous, casual leisure that develops organically from peer group affiliations'. Colin further stressed this when he told me how much forward planning is needed for him, as a wheelchair user, to spend time with his friends:

> Sonia [another member of YF] had this DJ gig in town. I really wanted to go, but I know how bad places are for me to get into, so I asked Sonia if it would be accessible. She said she wasn't sure but she'd ring up. We both rang them up actually, and they said it'd be fine. Anyway, I get there and they've got her DJ-ing in the basement! There's no way for me to get down. They gave me free drinks, but it's not quite the same sitting upstairs on your own. £40 taxi fare that was too. (Interview with Colin, 1st December 2011)

Colin alerts us to the daily consequences of exclusion arising from physical inaccessibility. It shows a tokenistic culture of access: the 'harsh paradox of the inaccessible labelled accessible' (Titchkosky 2011: 76–7). As Reeve (2012) highlights, even when physical access is granted separate back-street entrances or arrangements that provide only limited access to space do little for young disabled people's self-worth. Murray's (2002) young disabled participants stressed that spending time with their friends was more important than the particular activities they did together. Similarly, the pub apologetically offering Colin free drinks was little compensation for being excluded from his social circle.

84

For Colin, the £40 taxi fare adds insult to injury and highlights another plight in the lives of disabled young people: a lack of accessible public transport (Murray 2002). Partly due to inaccessible public transport, and partly resulting from what Colin considers his parents' over-protective attitudes (discussed in Chapter 5), Colin is, at great financial cost, reliant on taxis for transport. Other pictures from the cameras workshop reflected participants' frustrations around public transport. Although all young people complained of barriers to accessing transport, the particular barriers faced varied; pictures showed, for example, the large gaps between a station platform and a train; illustrating the most documented problem of the inaccessibility of public transport to people with physical impairments (see Wilson 2003 for an overview). Less widely considered, however, is the use of public transport for those with sensory and/ or intellectual impairments (Lavery, Knox and Slevin 1997; Mathers 2010). A picture of a speaker at a train station was taken by Ahmed, who has a hearing impairment. Ahmed complained of not being able to hear announcements. Another participant photographed a busy escalator; he said it was overwhelming and difficult. Many pictures also showed the confusing organisation of timetables. Participants thought this was particularly problematic for people with intellectual impairments, but that simplifying them could benefit everyone.

Intersectionality, Access and Mr Reasonable

These concerns which were captured from my fieldwork with young disabled people resonate with complaints of adult participants with intellectual impairments (Mathers 2010). Murray (2002) argues, however, that the accessibility of public transport may be more pertinent to disabled young people than adults, as young people are generally more reliant on public transport to get around (although she notes that not all disabled adults have the option of private vehicles). In fact, these complaints around public transport are probably feelings many of us – young, old, disabled, non-disabled – can empathise with. Stepping on the train with heavy bags in rush hour can be problematic for any number of people; not catching an announcement in a noisy station causes problems for those with and without hearing impairments; complicated timetabling has left me confused many a time. Access issues have come to be 'about disability' and concern 'disabled people'. We forget, however, that 'questions of access can arise for anyone, at any time, and anywhere for innumerable reasons' (Titchkosky 2011: 4).

Here I do not deny that the built environment prioritises some forms of embodiment over others. It is important to remember, however, that the built environment is part of, rather than separate from, socio-cultural-political contexts. The built environment, therefore, is wrapped up in myriad other ways that access is allowed or denied and must be interrogated through an intersectional lens. Access may, for example, arise in relation to gender. For some Muslim women a swimming pool where men are present would be inaccessible, or trans* people may require access to a gender neutral bathroom (in Chapter 6 I follow Kafer (2013) in considering toilets as a place to theorise relations between gender and disability access further). A lack of finance may stop you accessing a place, or one's particular faith/age and/or relation to alcohol may mean you cannot enter a space serving alcohol (see http://livingnotexisting.org/). Access may be denied due to the passport one holds which doesn't allow immigration to a particular country, or because you feel inadequate or unsafe within a particular space, or because systemic racism prevents you from accessing a particular job. Some of these in/exclusions are reflected more overtly in the built environment than others. Nevertheless, by being allowed access, the body and mind positioned as 'able'(which is always also intertwined with race, sexuality, gender, class global location and so on) is made invisible, as a lack of attention is paid to it.

Through this process the 'able' body is also rendered *reasonable*. In contrast, those to whom access is denied, are deemed unreasonable (Titchkosky 2011). Their invisibility may function, yet it functions differently, as they are excluded from *appearing* in certain spaces. Through identity political battles disabled people have demanded, for good reason, that they should not be excluded from any aspect of life. Arguably, this is one reason access issues have come to be 'about disability' (Titchkosky 2011). Yet, the continual 'conflation between the radical diversity of embodiment and the single iconic figure of the wheelchair user' (Titchkosky 2011: 81) means that access is often narrowed to simply stand for installing ramps for those who use wheelchairs (Russell 1998; Titchkosky 2011). This can result in tokenistic 'access' arrangements that prove problematic for disabled people such as Colin – you can come into the pub, but cannot access the gig.

We discussed access in relation to Britain's Equality Act 2010 in Chapter 1; let us think about this again now, in relation to public transport. According to the *Equality Act 2010*, disabled people using public transport '… have a right to reasonable adjustments. This can include providing timetables or other information in an accessible format, where it is reasonable for the transport provider to provide it' (DirectGov 2011). This seems good: we have, as Russell (1998) calls for, gone 'beyond ramps'. Yet there is a loophole: we say hello again to our friend Mr Reasonable. The demand of access must be a 'reasonable' one. We know from the social model that the problem is of inaccessible working practices and environments, not one of individual bodies (Oliver 1990). Yet, Mr Reasonable's ableist response to the question of access is to individualise: 'you cannot access work due to disability. But, as we are Reasonable Men, we will meet your individual access demands, if they too are Reasonable'. Whether or not demands are deemed to be reasonable, however, in having to individually demand access, self/Other relations are sustained. As Titchkosky (2011: 77) tells us, seeking reason for demands of accessibility means that 'whether or not the reasons for lack of access are judged good or bad, the social activity of people seeking reasons fosters the sensibility that lack of access is reasonable'. As a result, the bodies of those for whom work remains inaccessible, are deemed unreasonable; '"naturally" a problem for some spaces' (Titchkosky 2011: 35). The dyad between reasonable and unreasonable bodies functions to confirm our sense of normalcy.

Titchkosky (2011: 90) asks us not to think of access as just a demand, but to use questions of access to imagine 'access as a space [...] where questions of embodiment can be pursued'. We have seen that young disabled people are denied access to the same spaces as their non-disabled peers. A lack of access to public transport and the physical inaccessibility of buildings are only two ways that this exclusion functions. In Chapter 4, for example, we saw that Colin and Gabby from YF thought medical perspectives of disability influence their parents' perception of them as 'more vulnerable' than their non-disabled siblings and restricts what they are able to do (Hughes et al. 2005; Murray 2002; Priestley 2003). Furthermore, it has been recognised in literature that the practical need for physical assistance, usually provided by non-disabled adults, also prevents young disabled people accessing youth-only spaces (Gibson, Carnevale and King 2012; Hughes et al. 2005; Murray 2002; Priestley 2003; Wickenden 2010). We see then the need to continue fighting for disabled young people's access to space alongside their peers. Yet, I want to complicate this notion of access, by asking what conditions allow disabled young people's exclusion to space and activities on a par with their peers to appear reasonable? What is it that renders disabled young people 'naturally' 'exclude-able types' (Titchkosky 2003: 518) within so-imagined 'youthful' spaces? To consider this, I turn to some classic debates and texts from youth subcultural studies, and once again turn my attention to discourse.

Young People as Problems

In *Learning to Labour*, Willis (1977) engages with a group of lads in a secondary modern school. Willis' lads had little motivation for the formal lessons of the school, bragging about their avoidance of work. However, Willis highlights that their main aim was not to physically remove themselves from the school. There was little need, as they had other ways of ensuring their days were self-directed. The school used on their own terms was an interesting place to 'be with the lads'. Willis shows that the lads' defiance of school timeframes meant they were written-off early by staff and other students. Rather than considering the school system as unmeaningful to these students' social and cultural positions, those around the lads considered them as dangerous and disruptive annoyances. Like the aim of much youth subcultural work, through telling and theorising these lads' stories, Willis aimed to reposition them, not as dangerous and disruptive results of passive market appropriation, but as an active challenge to cultural and political hegemony (Hodkinson 2008).

In the late 1970s and early 1980s, however, criticisms emerged that youth subcultural researchers, such as Willis, were focusing exclusively on public displays of white, male youth; excluding the more private, but just as 'real' identity-forming experiences happening behind closed doors (Dorn and South 1999; McRobbie 1980, 1990; Rattansi and Phoenix 2005). McRobbie and Garber (2000) highlighted that youth subcultural researchers were drawing on what were new theories of deviance, which considered so-called deviant activity within wider societal and cultural practices. They argued that, with the possible exception of sexual deviance, girls and women were not considered excitingly deviant enough to be celebrated within these frameworks. Yet, disability remains missing from such critiques. Indeed, if we consider the situation of disabled young people, often construed as passive (see Chapter 1), and constricted to private spheres (Hughes et al. 2005), disability becomes conspicuous by its absence. Rather than account for the missing analysis of 'disability' in these older texts, or indeed trying to 'bring up to date' youth subcultural accounts by searching for 'disability' within more recent engagement, I want to consider what some of this old work can teach us about disabled young people's positioning in relation to youth culture today. What if Willis' lads had not been working-class white young men, but disabled young people refusing to conform to normative rules, structures and timeframes? How would they have been thought of by teachers and other students then? I recorded the following in my research diary, after meeting 13-year-old Treeman in art group Boom:

> Treeman has a strong Islamic faith. He makes the most out of Boom: using it to pursue his personal interests in languages and dentistry (the latter being one of his career aspirations). He regularly breaks away from his art to teach others the Arabic alphabet, or to squeeze remnants of high-school language lessons from members of staff. Another way Treeman furthers his interest in languages is to watch cartoons in a variety of languages on YouTube; ensuring he has time at the end of sessions to use Boom's computers. When Gareth's Mum, a doctor, arrives, Treeman fires questions at her about teeth. (Research diary, 12th October 2011, first Boom session)

Willis (1977) argues that the lads' rejection of the school was not without purpose. Rather, it was 'an aspect of [the lads'] immediate identity and self-direction. Time is used for the preservation of a state – being with "the lads" – not for the achievement of a goal – qualifications' (29). In the quote above Treeman displays his own strategies of claiming back time from the (semi)formal structure imposed by Boom and myself, in favour of his own here-and-now priorities, interests and learning. This philosophy to education was reflected in a piece of artwork Treeman created called 'a future day in the life of Treeman'. In this artwork we see that, given free rein to do as he liked, Treeman would study languages in the morning, and in the afternoon learn about time and camera light. This learning would not take place in school. Spanish would be taught in Spain, by a Spanish woman who (as Treeman put it in an interview) 'does not speak Arabic, Hebrew, English, French or Dutch, but only Spanish'. Treeman's days of learning would be punctuated with activities he enjoyed: going to soft play, mosque and feeding chickens. Learning would be tailored to suit his interests, taking place at times satisfying him. Furthermore, it is a philosophy of education which Treeman employs during Boom. Yet, like Willis' (1977) lads, when Treeman refuses imposed structures and timeframes, instead adopting his own philosophy of education, he is not praised for his desire to teach and learn, but conceived as a problem. However, rather than a rebellious, dangerous and disruptive overactive problem like Willis' (1977) lads, Treeman's refusal to conform is read as a 'disability problem'. This 'disability problem' renders Treeman the decidedly less exciting and glamorous problem of impairment and passivity. After my second session with Boom Treeman's story continues:

> Treeman was telling me about sharks' teeth today. It was cool. I got quite into the discussion, only momentarily finding it weird that [member of staff] kept changing the subject. I figured she just wasn't interested. Later she pulled me to one-side, and told me not to talk to Treeman about teeth, apparently an instruction passed on from his mother, on the advice of his school. (Research diary, 19th October 2011, second Boom session)

It is not that young disabled people lack agency, argue Hughes et al. (2005: 7), but that formal, segregated leisure schemes attempt to create 'docile subjects'. Forbidding Treeman from talking about teeth is an attempt to render him docile. It is, I would argue, an act of what Deal (2007) terms, 'aversive disablism': subtle prejudice which, although harmful, is often carried out unintentionally, perhaps even with good intentions. Boom staff, the teacher and Treeman's mother were all acting on the advice of those positioned as 'expert professionals'. As Freyja put it at a conference around independent living (discussed in Chapter 3), it exemplifies an 'it's for your own good attitude [that] disabled people face on a daily basis'.

To consider Treeman's situation further I introduce more CDS literature. I also (somewhat cautiously) share with you Treeman's diagnosis of autism. In their paper *Reading Rosie*, Goodley and Runswick-Cole (2012: 56) introduce us to 11-year-old Rosie, who also has a diagnosis of autism. They write accounts of Rosie's life through four different lenses: 1) a medically based the 'autism canon';[1] 2) a social model perspective; 3) the Nordic relational model of disability; and 4) a socio-cultural lens. It is the 'autism canon' which resonates most closely with the particular positioning Treeman is given in Boom. *Reading Rosie* through the 'autism canon' Goodley and Runswick-Cole write:

> As well as obsessing about Kitty, her new toy, [Rosie] also shows an obsessive interest in Goodies DVDs and Greek myths. Rosie has an impressive knowledge of vocabulary on the topic of Greek myths, however, this seemingly developed area of competence is a product of her fascination with mythology and should not distract from an understanding of the devastating impact of autism and learning difficulty on her life. (Goodley and Runswick-Cole 2012: 60)

Rather than a logical conclusion of his ambition to become a dentist, the medically-based autism canon makes Treeman's interest in teeth an obsession; a 'symptom' of his impairment label which it is desirable to solve. The solution is to render Treeman docile by refusing to acknowledge talk about teeth, arguably with the intention of guiding him from an unreasonable disability problem, to normative, reasonable adulthood.

After they have 'read Rosie', Goodley and Runswick-Cole (2012: 63) write that they 'see Rosie as a postmodern child, a child of which many stories can be told'. They ask us to consider our own readings and writings of disabled children. When youth subcultural researchers argue that young people are not passively appropriated by markets, but actively engaged within and shaping them (Hall and Jefferson 2006; McRobbie 2005) they attempt to tell different stories about young people. When Willis (1977: 29) highlights the purpose of the lads' non-conformist attitudes as 'an aspect of [the lads'] immediate identity and self-direction', he is telling a different story to the one imagined by the teachers and other students. Telling different stories about 'disability' is one of the aims of disability studies; indeed, this book aims to tell different stories about 'youth', 'disability' and 'young disabled

---

1   When Goodley and Runswick-Cole (2012) write of the 'autism canon', they conceptualise this as the dominant, medically diagnosed/clinical label. It should be noted, however, that other people identifying as autistic and/or neurodiverse have taken and resignified 'autism' in different ways.

people'. It could (perhaps legitimately) be argued that by equating Willis' (1977) and Treeman's stories, I have crudely compared two very different contexts. I use the stories, however, to highlight the different ways people are conceptualised as problems, dependent upon identity. The problem of Willis' (1977) non-conformist white, male working-class youth is one of over-activity. The problem of Treeman, a non-conformist disabled youth is a problem of impairment, specifically intellectual impairment, which is often either associated with passivity, or rendered so with medication (Timimi, Gardner and McCabe 2010). We saw in Chapter 1 the danger of being construed as passive. If we consider young disabled people's positioning as passive youth (Slater 2013) alongside feminist subcultural critiques, it is unsurprising that disability was not on the cards of youth subcultural researchers (Baron, Riddell and Wilson 1999; Butler 1998). Furthermore, such a positioning contributes to the ableist ideologies and systems, reflected in design, which mean disabled young people continue to be 'unexpected participants' (Titchkosky 2011) within spaces (clubs, public transport, pubs and so on) that their peers might have access to today.

If we continue with Treeman's story, however, we are once again reminded that 'disabled people are not simply passive victims of [...] disablism – many exercise agency and resist' (Reeve 2002: 493). As fieldwork with Boom continued, not being able to talk to Treeman about teeth became more ridiculous. Treeman was sure from day one that a dentist would be the main feature of his final art piece, yet staff kept referring to it as 'the building'. In my penultimate session with Boom I recorded the following:

> Hurrah! Today I witnessed a momentous event! Whilst staff were distracted, Treeman sneakily constructed a dentist sign which is now stuck proudly on his DENTIST (not building!) in his ideal world! (Research diary, 7th December 2011, Boom ninth session)

Treeman wins out!! Or ... have I gone too far in my celebrations? Is Treeman's dental sign a signal for celebration when we consider all the confusing, contradictory, oppressive, constricting and exclusionary messages delivered around youth and disability? Some argue that youth subcultural researchers allowed for too much agency: ignoring regulation, constraint, and the perpetuation of injustices, thus, 'adumbrat[ing] the need for complex understanding of power by suggesting it can be too easily opposed, countered or thrown off by so-called active agents' (McRobbie 2005: 86). My celebration of Treeman's dental sign could be illustrative of this. After all, through the camera lenses of young people at YF and the words of Meow at the beginning of this chapter, we saw some of the barriers young disabled people face in accessing 'youthful spaces'.

Figure 5.1   The dentist in Treeman from Boom's final art piece

I take note from Goodley (1999: 41, my emphasis), however, when he writes, 'two of the main purposes of disability research are first, to unmask the processes of disablement, and second, to pinpoint how resilience is borne out of these exclusionary environments … experts of disablement [such as Treeman] can alert us to the characteristics of disabling environments *and* point us to the origins of resilience'. Therefore, as part of the fight for disabled young people's right to access the same spaces as their non-disabled peers, I wonder whether rather than assume young disabled people are not a part of youth culture (hence rendering them passive), it would be more useful to question the meanings we attribute to both 'disability' and 'youth culture'. An aim of this book is to explore the complicated ways 'youth' is discursively constructed, and the equally complex ways disabled people are rooted by and simultaneously challenge dominant discourses of disability. To speak unquestionably of a 'youth culture' is to deny the multiplicity of ways young people 'do' 'being young'; hence further distancing young disabled people from discourses of youth (Slater 2012). This perhaps adds to discourses that make young disabled people appear as reasonably excludable (Titchkosky 2003) from spaces accessible to their non-disabled peers. I turn now then to show disabled young people actively negotiating youth cultural spaces.

'Doing Youth'

Before I begin this section, I reassert a statement made in the introduction to this chapter. I am in no doubt that young disabled people are accessing a variety of youth (sub)cultures, and that technology has changed young people's relationships with young subcultural space. Yet, rather than engage with spaces we may explicitly consider subcultural, in this chapter I want to question assumptions around what a youth cultural space looks like by engaging with the negotiations made by the particular young people I spent time with, within the spaces they had access to. I do this here through further engagement with Meow from Boom. Out of all my participants, the worries about lack of access to adult-free arenas, and therefore 'youth culture', were arguably most applicable to those at Boom. Boom is an art group funded by the UK government initiative, *Aiming High for Disabled Children*. Unlike the other two research contexts, Boom is run for, rather than by, disabled people. Out of all strands of my research, it is most typical of the kinds of segregated schemes Hughes et al. (2005) argue separate disabled youth from their non-disabled peers. Furthermore, Boom is specifically for those with labels of intellectual impairment, who it has been argued: a) are most readily left aside in disability politics and research (Goodley 2001); and b) have less access to youth-only spaces than those with physical impairments (Murray 2002). As a group easily positioned as an 'exclude-able type' (Titchkosky 2003: 518) from 'youth culture', the young people in Boom therefore have the most to teach me about the possible exclusionary nature of youth culture (Goodley 1999).

McRobbie (2000: 45) writes that 'only by working away from the more transparent or mainstream youth and in [her] case working class female youth, is it possible to piece together and understand girl's culture'. Although members of Boom (unlike in other research contexts) did not talk to me about being *disabled* people, they did assert themselves as *youth*. Considering the way young people 'did' 'being young people' can help us 'work away from more transparent or mainstream youth' (McRobbie 2000: 45). However, whereas McRobbie tries to '*piece together* and *understand* girls' culture' (McRobbie 2000, my emphasis), I instead consider the ways young disabled people negotiate 'youth' in order to *pull apart* and help us *expand* notions of youth culture.

We saw earlier Meow asserting herself as youth as she declared that nightclubs were 'not for old people'. Meow specifies that nightclubs, along with funfairs and shopping centres are places she would like to spend time. Although Meow's barriers to accessing these spaces may not spring to mind under the 'single iconic figure of the wheelchair user' (Titchkosky 2011: 81), we've seen the attitudinal, financial and informational barriers she may face in accessing these spaces as a young woman labelled with intellectual impairments

(Murray 2002). However, like the young disabled people in Murray's (2002) study, Meow emphasised that it was more important for her to generally 'hang out' with friends than take part in any particular activity. Although Meow spoke seriously of wanting to work with children when she was older, she was aware that in the current political climate it was particularly difficult to get a job. This would not be a problem in her ideal world, in response to the question, 'How does the future person spend their day? Do they have a job? Go to school?' Meow writes, 'They do not go to school or have a job. They just relax'. I asked Meow to expand:

[Jenny]: 'What do they do if they don't go to school or have a job?'

[Meow]: 'You know, just relax. Be lazy. You don't always have to be doing something – what about just doing nothing with your mates'.

(Interview with Meow, 10th October 2011)

An argument employed to defend young people demonised as (overactive) hoodies and hooligans is that we cannot blame young people for hanging around on streets when there is little choice of alternative spaces (such as youth clubs) for them to spend time (Topping 2011). We saw in Chapter 2, that there are diminishing numbers of services for young people, and this concerned members of YF quoted at the beginning of this chapter. Conversely, however, disability studies texts often point to another, almost oppositional problem; disabled young people have less casual 'hanging out' time than their non-disabled peers (Baron et al. 1999; Goodley and Runswick-Cole 2010; Hughes 2005; Priestley 2003). Priestley (2003) highlights that disabled young people's leisure time is often highly structured, concerned not with 'leisure' but filling in time, preparing for a meaningful life without work, giving the family a break and/or managing undesirable behaviour. Spaces which are far-flung from those we may consider part of youth culture. In concurrence with the above scholars, Meow emphasised to me the importance of having time to 'do nothing with her mates'. As a young woman with a label of intellectual impairment in a segregated scheme, Meow is arguably representative of those most often denied this freedom (Hughes et al. 2005; Murray 2002; Priestley 2003).

In *The Culture of Working Class Girls* McRobbie (2000) makes similar points along the axis of gender that I make along axis of disability. She notes that girls had more structure imposed on their lives than their male peers. Furthermore, their perceived vulnerability meant they had less 'freedom' to hang around on the streets. There was an expectation on McRobbie's girls to cook their families' evening meals which then won them time at the local youth club, before conforming to a 10.30pm curfew. Similarly to the structuring of leisure for Boom members, the school, family and youth club worked to shape McRobbie's (2000) girls' lives in particular gendered ways. To stop at an analysis that used Boom only as an example of the overly-structured lives of young disabled people, however, would be to do a disservice to those involved (staff and young people). Boom offered different things to different young people. For some members, particularly US1234 and Gareth, who both aspire to careers as artists, the group's main benefit was furthering their artistic capabilities; yet this was not the case for all involved. We saw how Treeman made the most of his time by pursuing his personal interests. Meow seemed to gain greatest pleasure from the social aspects of the group. Meow would often declare, 'I'm not going to do anything today; I'm just going to relax'. Appreciative that young people enjoyed the group for different reasons, the staff (some more than others) were not pushy in getting the young people 'on task', and would usually respond by asking Meow about her day at college, 'been a busy one, has it?' 'Yeah', Meow would reply, sighing, sometimes playfully adding, '... and I'm just a lazy teenager'.

McRobbie (2000: 45) writes that 'the 'cultural' is always a site for struggle and conflict', and that on first glance her group of working class girls seemed to have less of a culture of opposition and resistance to that usually documented by youth subcultural researchers concerned with male youth. Neither did I see overt opposition coming from members of Boom. Yet McRobbie (2000) points out that having less freedom from adult surveillance did not mean girls unquestionably accepted what was presumed of them – and neither did it for those at Boom. Rather, the girls' defiance emerged as '"gentle" undermining [and] subtle redefinition' (McRobbie 2000: 53). McRobbie notes that whereas boys were more likely to skip school and avoid the youth club, the girls had their own techniques of claiming time for themselves: they attended but did not 'participate' in youth club activities; 'they were *in* school but not *at* the school' (McRobbie 2000, original italics). A similar analysis could be made of Meow's time in Boom. Structural barriers, working along the axis of disability (and perhaps also gender, class and so on), influence how she spent her time. Nevertheless, like Treeman, Meow had her own strategies of making Boom meaningful, and claiming time from the (semi)formal structures it imposed.

After entering and asserting her desire to 'do nothing' Meow would often continue to 'do nothing' ... at least, this is how it was seen by Boom staff who would joke with Meow about her laziness. In 1979 Corrigan (2006) looked at what a group of teenage lads meant when they spoke of 'doing nothing' on the street. Corrigan argues that for the lads, 'doing nothing' was more complex than merely a lack of options. 'Doing nothing' was about passing time together through talk and the exchange of stories. 'Doing nothing' was a time of ideas. He argues that although a lens of adulthood casts 'doing nothing' 'as an endless waste of time, an absence of purpose' for the young people 'doing nothing' was in fact 'full of incident' (Corrigan 2006: 84). Similarly, although Meow was seen as 'doing nothing' it was in fact quite the opposite. Like Corrigan's lads, she would talk and exchange stories; joking with and playfully teasing myself and Boom staff, whilst chatting to other young people. Furthermore, Corrigan poses that the boys did not choose to 'do nothing' on the street because the street was the most exciting place they could conceive. However, out of their limited options (the lone pursuits of home or the humdrum of the youth club) it offered most chance of something happening in the future. Similarly, Meow's choices of how she spent her time were limited. Maybe (although it was never directly expressed), she would have preferred a less formal social setting if given the choice. Nevertheless, she made the most of her time at Boom. By expressing her desire to 'do nothing' Meow proclaims her agency to make her own decisions away from the imposed routines of school/college/work, and indeed, Boom. Like McRobbie's (2000: 64) girls, she was often '*in* Boom, but not *at* Boom'. Conversely, in order to associate herself with 'youth', Meow asserts her passivity (being a lazy teenager, enjoying 'doing nothing'), yet these assertions are in themselves actively and playfully demonstrating her agency through their desire to mark herself as a young person, separate to the rat race of adulthood. As Corrigan (2006) teaches us, although frowned upon as laziness and passivity, 'doing nothing' can be young people's lively engagement with one-another and the world around them: one can be an active agent, in what could, on the surface, be considered their most 'passive' of activities.

So, Can You Go Clubbing with Your Mum and Dad?

My point in the latter half of this chapter hasn't been to deny the need to continue fighting for disabled young people to have access to the same spaces as their peers. To the contrary in fact, the point has been try unpick some of the reasons it may continually be deemed *reasonable* to exclude disabled young people from such spaces; exclusion which manifests itself both in the built environment, but also in paternalistic attitudes, policy documents and so on, all of which are part of larger cultures of ableism. Whereas McRobbie tries to '*piece together* and *understand* girls culture' (McRobbie 2000, my emphasis), in the latter half of this chapter I have instead considered the ways young disabled people negotiate 'youth' in order to *pull apart* and help us *expand* notions of youth culture. I agree with McRobbie (2000) that culture involves moments of struggle; we see these taking place as disabled youth negotiate their time and relationships in Boom. I also follow McRobbie (1990: 45) when she writes that 'culture is about the prestructured but still essentially expressive and creative capacities of the group in question'. We have seen the expressive and creative capacities of young people in Boom. These were illustrated to me not just through their artwork, but also through their negotiations and resistance within prestructured arrangements that are, undoubtedly, imposed upon their lives (Hughes et al. 2005). Furthermore, we have witnessed disabled young people actively asserting themselves as 'youth'. The problem is then twofold. I again reiterate that I do not deny young disabled people's exclusion from spaces and pursuits on par with their non-disabled peers; disablist social oppression which needs to be addressed. However, there are other issues at play which separate disabled young people from discourses of youth: narrow, misleading and ableist conceptions of youth culture influencing perceptions of what it is to be young, meaning disabled youth's lack of access to youth culture continues to appear reasonable (Titchkosky 2011). Although we must continue to fight for young disabled people's access to the same spaces as their non-disabled peers, I argue that we cannot simply demand young people's access to 'youth culture'. 'Culture' is not a 'thing' but a series of relationships: 'at least in part as the product of collective human praxis' (Willis 1977: 4). I have shown that disabled young people are already active players within this. If ableist conceptions, as we have seen, have meant chronologically *young* disabled people's negotiations, struggles and sites of conflict are not recognised within youth cultural discourse, what is it that makes normative conceptions of 'youth culture', 'youthful'?

Chapter 6 continues to consider the relationship between disability and youthfulness, but this time via questions of gender, sexuality and the body.

Chapter 6
Dis/abled Youth, Bodies, Femininity and Sexuality: Having Difficult Conversations

This chapter thinks about youth as embodied, gendered and sexualised by engaging with queer, feminist and feminist-disability texts, alongside stories of young disabled women who took part in my fieldwork. The stories of young women are prominent in this chapter. Perhaps due to the close friendships I developed with young women, conversations of gender and sexuality during fieldwork arose mainly with women. This is not to say that the issues weren't pertinent for young men. Furthermore, all the women I spent time with were cis gendered. This is not to deny experiences of gender, sexuality and the body of trans*[1] women. Rather, by chance, it was only cis identifying women that ended up part of my research. As will be explored through this chapter, issues of bodies and bodily ideals remain heavily gendered, and more work needs to be done which explores disabled trans* people's experiences.

I begin by introducing you to Lotta and Princess Bella, two of the young women that attended Boom, through a pen portrait sketched after our first meeting:

Lotta and Bella didn't just walk in, they waltzed in. They've got style! 13-year-old Lotta's 'look' sits something between Lady Gaga and Lily Allen. She pulled off her leopard print hat to reveal an asymmetrical haircut, working with her denim shorts and mismatched Converse trainers. This girl's cool! Far too cool for the likes of me: she wasn't particularly interested in talking, wanting to knuckle down and get on with things. 16-year-old Bella, Lotta's older sister, was more up for a chat. She tells me that she and Lotta share a bedroom, and they've got different ideas about how it should look. The family are moving house soon, where Bella will have her own room which she'll paint pink with her Mum. I get the impression of a feminist 'girls-together' family. Five sisters,

---

1   I precede the word 'trans' with a * to indicate that by trans* I am not only referring to those who identify as transgender, but those who do not identify as a cis man or woman (this includes, amongst others, people that identify as non-binary, genderqueer and genderless).

Mum (who stays for the session), and an assortment of pets – no mention of Dad. Both girls have the label of intellectual impairment. Unlike Lotta, Bella's impairment is visible. Bella does the moody teenager thing incredibly well! It seems in her cool arty family she's already done everything I had on offer. Eventually, I persuaded her to have a look at the '*Report from the Future*' and think about where she wants to take her ideas from there. (Research diary, 7th December 2012, Boom)

The *Report from the Future* booklets were booklets I designed for young people in Boom to sketch out their ideas for a final 'best ever future world' art piece. They opened with the text: 'Welcome time traveller. Your mission: You have travelled forward in time to a world that is just as you like it. Here, everything is just as you wish. It is your best-ever future world. Please use this book to report back on what you find'. They then asked young people questions about what they found in their best-ever future world, including: you have arrived in your best-ever future world, what do you see? You meet someone from your best-ever future world, what do they look like? Where does the future person live? Space was left for young people to draw, stick or write their answers, which they were encouraged to approach the task in their preferred format. I sat with Bella and Lotta while they filled in their 'Report from the Future' booklet. My research diary continues:

Lotta chose the age of her time travelling avatar to be '10, 954 (but don't have wrinkles)'. Lotta was aiming this tease at her Mum, who sat across the table from her. Later Bella got to the question which asked her to describe what she saw stepping out of her time machine. She drew a woman in a red dress, heels and a crown, with exaggerated red lipstick, large circles of blusher and big eyes with predominant eye-lashes (Figure 5.1). I asked Bella if the picture was of her, the time traveller, or someone that lived in the future world. I was shocked when she told me it could never be her because she was too 'fat and ugly', but this drawing was what women were meant to look like. (Research diary, 7th December 2012, Boom)

Caught off-guard in a busy room with lots of noise, movement and mess, my response to Bella was to repeat what I have experienced with groups of 'girl friends' before. I told Bella 'not to be silly'; of course she was not 'fat' or 'ugly'. Perhaps (although I am sceptical), at this moment my response offered temporary assurance to Bella of her place within commodified discourses of 'the body beautiful'. On reflection, however, I was cross about the *reasonableness* of my reply: as, through its normativity, I had failed to challenge the status-quo. I didn't, for example, try to discuss the diversity of bodies; issues around gender stereotypes; the commodified expectations on women to look a certain way.

Figure 6.1   Princess Bella from Boom's illustration of what she sees in her future world

Nor did I talk to Bella about the place of capitalism and 'normal' within discourses of gendered and sexualised bodily ideals; never mind how 'disability' or 'youth' are entwined within all of this. One may argue that this was neither the time nor place for such conversations (although this leads me to think – when is?). Nevertheless, the message that was conveyed here was problematic: I confirmed that 'fat and ugly' are real things that were bad … but that it was ok, because they were things that Bella wasn't.

My response above in fact illustrates what activist Mia Mingus (2011) may call an 'easy conversation'. Taking a deeply intersectional approach to her activism, Mingus (2011) writes as 'a queer, disabled, Korean woman, transracial/ transnational adoptee, raised in a US territory in the Caribbean'. Identities, she tells us which are equally as important as each other. In an essay called *Moving Toward the Ugly: A Politic Beyond Desirability*, she asks what it would mean to shift our desires 'from [easy] conversations of beauty and easy and me, to [difficult conversations of] ugly and magnificence and we'. In this chapter I attempt to work through this question, spurred by Mingus to think about the potential consequences of continuing to choose 'easy conversations' for those whose bodies don't comply with Mr Reasonable's norms. Recognising identities as profoundly embodied I begin with a discussion of femininity in relation to Bella's remarks about 'fat' and 'ugly'. This leads me to think about discourses of ab/normal bodies. Drawing on Mingus (2011), I contextualise such discourse within cultures of violence, and use ableism as a lens to interrogate such violence at the border zone of youth (Lesko 2012). Despite the doom and gloom, however, I also share stories of resistance to this oppressive, dangerous and violent border zone.

'Fat and Ugly': Difficult Conversations of Femininity

It has been acknowledged that remaining 'youthful' is an expectation of the (predominantly) female body (Featherstone 1982; Heiss 2011; Slater 2012). When Lotta above quips that she would be very old, but have no wrinkles, she demonstrates her awareness of this expectation. Elsewhere I have thought about the requirement to buy into a 'youth-beauty-thing' by terming the implicit relationship between youth and the 'body beautiful', 'youth for sale'; a depiction that, as we will see through this chapter, has been commodified and fetishised so it is unrepresentative of young people's lives (Slater 2012, 2013). Google 'stay youthful' and you're bombarded with 'tips' and 'secrets' to 'staying young'/ 'keeping your body young'/'remaining young and beautiful'; most of which have women as their main target audience, and come with an expectation to buy into a market of products, services and systems which will make us 'happier', 'healthier' and 'complete' (Davis 2002). In a study exploring 'aging women's' attempts at remaining 'youthful', participants reported a desire to attract a romantic partner, fighting age-related invisibility and employment-related ageism as reasons to retain a 'youthful' appearance (Clarke and Griffin 2008).

Furthermore, a project focused on age-based discrimination in the financial sector concluded that 'women were more likely than men to experience ageist attitudes concerning appearance or sexuality' (C. Duncan and Loretto 2004: 95). Bordo (1993) points out that when discussed, particularly with psychological and/or medical frameworks, studies of weight and body image usually focus on pathological accounts of 'eating disorders'. Yet, she argues that the 'preoccupation with fat, diet, and slenderness [...] may function as one of the most powerful normalising mechanisms of our century' (Bordo 1993: 186); and one that *all* women (and, to a lesser extent, men) are vulnerable to (Bordo 1993).

To muse over what form difficult conversations around bodies and 'youthfulness' may take we need to pay attention to the ideals of femininity and masculinity which bodily ideals rest upon. Bergman (2009: 139) writes that 'I look the same every day. I'm five feet nine inches tall, broad shouldered and white skinned – blue jeans and button-downs, boots or sandals. I wear glasses. All these things are true all the time, and yet even so I am only Fat in the normative, cultural, "Ew, gross, look at it jiggle" sense about a third of the time'. Bergman goes on to explain that despite identifying as a butch transgender man, he is sometimes taken for a man, and sometimes taken for a woman. His experiences of fatness alter dependent on the reading of his gender: as a man, he is 'a big dude, but not outside the norm'; when read as a woman, on the other hand, 'I am revolting' (Bergman 2009: 141). Bordo (1993) traces the weighted expectation put on the female body back to the mind/body dualism present in Western philosophical and theological thought. She explains that the body has been associated with femininity, and been thought of as separate from and often a burden to the mind: 'as animal, as appetite, as deceiver, as prison of the soul and confounder of its projects' (Bordo 1993: 3). Masculinity, on the other hand, has historically been associated with mind and reason (see Chapter 3). It is no mere coincidence that we have a *Mr*, rather than a Miss/Mrs/Ms Reasonable haunting this book. As a woman's survival has been dependent on male approval and her servicing and pleasuring of men, there has and continues to be a greater expectation on women to meet certain 'beauty' standards (Bordo 1993). It is important to remember, however, that this culture is not just coded by gender, but also by race, class, dis/ability, age, sexuality, global location and so on. Our Mr Reasonable, therefore, is not only male, but also non-disabled, cis gendered, white, heterosexual and from a Western European or North American country. Bordo (1993) uses the case of the muscular body to make this point. Whereas muscles have been associated with masculinity, and men's more muscular physique often cited as the 'naturalness' of difference between men and women, cultural constructions of muscles are also classed and raced. Classed, in that they are associated with the proletariat and manual work; and raced, as they are depicted 'in numerous film representations of sweating, glistening bodies, belonging to black slaves and prizefighters' (Bordo 1993: 195).

Mingus (2011) argues that ableism needs to be at the forefront of any discussion of bodies, as it cuts across these intersectional conversations. I first introduced the concept of ableism my letter to Mr Reasonable (see Introduction). According to Campbell (2009: 44) ableism is a 'network of beliefs, processes and practices that produces a particular kind of self and body (the corporeal standard) that is projected as the perfect, species-typical and therefore essential and fully human'. This corporeal standard isn't only reliant on the category of dis/ability, rather '[t]he nuances of ableism [...] are transcategorical, having specific cultural alignments with other factors such as race, gender, sexuality and coloniality' (Fiona Kumari Campbell 2012: 214). As Mingus explains:

> Ableism cuts across all of our movements because ableism dictates how bodies should function against a mythical norm – an able-bodied standard of white supremacy, heterosexism, sexism, economic exploitation, moral/religious beliefs, age and ability. Ableism set the stage for queer and trans people to be institutionalized as mentally disabled; for communities of color to be understood as less capable, smart and intelligent, therefore 'naturally' fit for slave labor; for women's bodies to be used to produce children, when, where and how men needed them; for people with disabilities to be seen as 'disposable' in a capitalist and exploitative culture because we are not seen as 'productive;' for immigrants to be thought of as a 'disease' that we must 'cure' because it is 'weakening' our country; for violence, cycles of poverty, lack of resources and war to be used as systematic tools to construct disability in communities and entire countries. (Mingus 2011)

Following Mingus, ableism then also dictates how young, female-read bodies[2] should function against a mythical-norm. As femininity is reliant upon ableism, and ableism is, to use Campbell's (2012: 214) words, 'transcategorical', paying attention to ableism also helps us to see that how young female-read bodies do and are allowed to function varies dependent upon other intersecting identities. When I write of 'femininity', then, I am conceptualising it not as a descriptor, but an ideological system, which *all* people are implicated and participate within (Bordo 1993; Butler 1999; Fisanick 2009). In *Gender Trouble*, Butler (1999) argues that gender is presented to us a binary male/female construct and heterosexual hegemony is shored-up through a reiterative and ritualistic performance of these roles. She calls this performativity: gender and sex are revealed not as 'natural', but acts materialised through performativity (Butler 1999). One performance expected of the female body is to remain 'youthful'

---

2 I distinguish here between female-read bodies and female-identifying people. As I will come to, female-identifying people not read as female, or male-identifying people not read as male, already challenge the dangerous binaries based upon gender.

(Slater 2012). Furthermore, femininity plays out not only along gendered, but also aged, raced, classed, sexualised and dis/abled axes of power. It is therefore read differently in different contexts. I pay particular attention to disabled women in this chapter, however, not to discount the (arguably increasing) expectation on men to perform 'body work'. Nor, to deny the intersecting relationships between transhistorical categories of race, gender, sexuality, dis/ability and so on. Rather, I focus on disabled women's experiences, firstly as these were the ways in which the young women that spoke to me about gender, sexuality and the body identified; and secondly, to acknowledge the complex and intersectionally dependent relationships between expected femininity and youthfulness, and the potential consequences of this (Slater 2012).

Such a commodified 'youthful' expectation is both moralised and rife with contradiction. As both Bergman's (2009) and Bella's stories make us aware, one expectation of the young female body, is to be thin (Bordo 1993; Heiss 2011). Fat scholars and activists have highlighted the contradictions in the multi-billion dollar weight-loss industry (Rothblum and Soloway 2009), citing examples such as the multinational consumer goods company, Unilever, owning both Ben & Jerry's ice-cream and the Slim Fast brand of 'diet foods'. These realisations clearly relate the bodily expectation of slenderness back to global capitalist markets. Yet, the message delivered is that those not meeting the ideal body (particularly in terms of thin/fat), are lazy, unproductive and irresponsible (Boero 2009). These depictions, in fact, are not so different to the depictions of disabled people discussed in Chapter 1 (Herndon 2003).

Herndon (2003) further explores the relationships between fat and disabled bodies. She points out that shaped by medicalisation and pathologisation, dominant cultural representations of 'fat' and 'disabled' bodies similarly serve to teach fat and disabled people that they are a drain on resources and an affront to aesthetic ideals (Herndon 2003). Herndon (2003) argues therefore that these depictions of fat and disabled bodies serve a purpose within (neo)liberal consumerist societies; acting as 'warning signs' and teaching those that are not (yet) disabled or fat, to avoid becoming one of 'them' (Herndon 2003; Shildrick 2009). As explained in Chapter 2, Foucault (1979) termed the relationships between the body and power, biopower. Although within (neo)liberalism there is a façade of expected activity, this activity is about economic market-based productivity within a culture that requires self-surveying and politically docile bodies. We see here that the marginalisation of fat and disabled bodies helps sustain self-surveying subjects ('watch your weight', 'stay healthy'), who are encouraged to be economically active to buy themselves 'thin'/'able' (Davis 2001; Rothblum and Soloway 2009). As blogger Geo July (2014) puts it, '[f]eeling like shit about whatever your specific issue […] is the result of a system SPECIFICALLY DESIGNED to make people feel like shit so they buy more stuff'.

Thinking back to Chapter 1, to be a citizen, one must be a consumer, and this consumerism dictates the ways in which we live in and feel about our bodies (Slater 2012). Bella's feels, for example, that she is 'too fat and ugly' to be what women should be.

Bodies and Violence

We have touched upon 'violence' in previous chapters. For Mingus (2011), to analyse the possible implications of bodily ideals we need to consider the violence in the lives of those that don't adhere to them. To understand Mingus' reasoning we need think beyond an understanding of violence as one-off acts, performed by individual people/bullies on individual victims, to instead think about the culture underpinning such violence (Friedman and Valenti 2008; Galtung 1990; Goodley and Runswick-Cole 2011). Following Galtung (1990) I am conceptualising cultural violence as a culture which allows for violent acts to seem 'normal', 'right' or, at least, 'not wrong'. To use an example: Freyja, one of my participants from Iceland writes of the difficulties she had in trying to buy clothes as a teenage girl wanting to 'fit in' with her peers. She describes these clothes as being made for the 'one and only girl body' (that was different to hers). This may not in itself be conceptualised as an act of violence; in fact, the argument may be made that clothes manufacturers are catering for 'the majority'. Yet, cultures of violence are particularly dangerous as they allow for Mr Reasonable to roll his eyes, tell us we're being oversensitive, or that it's 'just the way it is'. However, clothes only being made in certain shapes and sizes perpetuate the myth that some bodies are 'normal' and others are 'abnormal'. We therefore need to appreciate them as part of a violent culture that can result in violent acts.

Such bodily ideals, for example, lead Bella to tell me that she is 'too fat and ugly' to be what women should be. We can read Bella's assertion as a form of internalised oppression, resulting from psycho-emotional violence; a type of violence that undermines the psychological well-being of people, affecting what they can *be*, rather than just what they can *do* (Reeve 2002). Violent cultures also allowed for my own reasonable response that, in an attempt to reassure Bella, resulted in the Othering of people that aren't Bella; a response that in fact plays into violent cultures. Furthermore, feelings of inadequacy such as those Bella has, can have directly violent consequences (Reeve 2002). By direct violence, I mean embodied encounters of physical or psychological pain being inflicted from one body to another (Goodley and Runswick-Cole 2011). For example, exploring the self-esteem of women with physical impairments Hassouneh-Phillips and McNeff found:

> Women with high degrees of physical impairment are more likely to perceive themselves as sexually inadequate and unattractive than women with mild impairment. These negative perceptions, when combined with a strong desire to be partnered, increased women's vulnerability to getting into and staying in abusive relationships over time. (Hassouneh-Phillips and McNeff 2005: 227)

We begin to see that exploring the intersecting marginalisation of fat and disabled bodies, is not just illuminating (Herndon 2003), but urgent. However, much of the literature surrounding women and body image concerns non-disabled women.[3] We are perhaps not surprised by this: we have seen throughout this book that disability is often left aside in embodied and identity-based conversations (Davis 2002) (see Introduction and Chapter 2). Yet, within a culture of violence, this should not be considered a mere oversight, but an act of aversive disablism (Deal 2007) underpinned by dangerous biopolitical assumptions which position disabled people as Other, and outside of humanity. Similar racist ideas that women of colour are immune to standards of slenderness have also been posed in relation to women of colour (Bordo 1993); and there has been a tendency to believe that lesbians are also immune to pressures imposed from a masculine gaze (Atkins 1998). McCarthy (1998) highlights the prevailing view that disabled women (particularly with intellectual impairments) are in some way 'blessed' to not feel pressured to conform to Western conceptions of bodily norms. Perhaps unsurprisingly given the ableist culture, McCarthy's findings around the bodily satisfaction of women with labels of intellectual impairment showed quite the opposite – *all* the women found it difficult to say anything positive about their bodies. Moreover, McCarthy shows us that the dangers of not questioning what is considered 'normal' and 'ideal' are arguably greater for disabled women (and other women in equally powerless positions) due to unequal social positioning (see also, Calderbank 2000).

All the women in McCarthy's (1998) study were adults, and, unlike Bella and Lotta, all but one were living in either institutional or supported community

---

3   One way 'body image has been explored is though 'eating disorders'. As many 'eating disorders' are now incorporated into the 'Diagnostic and Statistical Manual of Mental Disorders', it should therefore be noted, that the assertion that most explorations of women and body image concern non-disabled women, depends to an extent on the perspective one takes on the relationship between 'disability/impairment' and 'mental health' (see Beresford 2002). However, when studies do consider young women with 'eating disorders', explicitly thinking of this in terms of 'disability', these are usually pathological accounts which is of course problematic, and not necessarily in line with the ways that the subjects of the text would conceptualise their own lives (Bordo 1993). To this end, I want to also note that the term 'eating disorder' is in itself problematic and may not be one that those given that label associate with.

settings with professional assistance. These systems perpetuated structural violence as the women had little control over their own bodies: from deciding when to wash and what clothes to wear, to what contraception they used. McCarthy poses that many of the issues the women had with their own bodies were a result of staff control and a lack of autonomy: attempts were made, through institutional processes, to make them passive pawns in their own lives (Hughes 2001). In the last chapter, we saw that Embla from the *Independent Living Centre* in Iceland, said that for her, 'independent living means being able to be a woman' (Haraldsdóttir and Sigurdardttir 2011: 7), and the stories McCarthy tells, contextualise this feeling:

> One woman said it was her keyworker's decision that she should diet, not her own. Another described the staff's efforts to control her eating in the following way: 'They won't let me have ice-cream, they say "you can't have this, you can't have that"'. They boss me around'. The irony was that this woman had, in fact, put on a lot of weight as a direct result of the medication which staff had prescribed and administered. (McCarthy 1998: 561)

Of course, these forms of violence – psycho-emotional, direct, structural and cultural – are not separate, but wrapped up and implicated in one-another, with some of them more easily 'seen' than others. For Butler (1999) we must also consider gender binaries as part of a culture of violence. Butler (1999: xxii) asks us to consider 'how presumptions about normative gender and sexuality determine in advance what will qualify as "human" and the "livable"?' For a life to be considered 'liveable' one must be considered an intelligible subject, and for Butler (1999: 22) '"persons" only become intelligible through becoming gendered in conformity with recognizable standards of gender intelligibility'. She argues that the naturalisation of gender binaries means oppressing people who do not fit within such a binary construct. This includes trans* people who do not identify with the gender they were assigned at birth. However, as gender constructs dictate the perceptions of ab/normal sexuality, gender policing also affects those who are cis gender but do not conform to match normative constructs of heterosexuality (Payne and Smith 2012). As Horn (2007: 329) points out, for example, homophobic bullying and violence is often not 'based solely on sexual orientation, but rather from judgments about perceived tendencies to engage in forms of expression that run counter to gender conventions'.

McRuer (2006a, 2006b) puts Butler to work by considering the ableism inherent to discourses of gender intelligibility. He argues that as 'gender' and 'ability' are wrapped up and implicated in one-another disabled people are continually read outside of normative discourses of gender and sexuality, despite how they may identify in terms of gender and sexuality. As he writes:

… people with disabilities are often understood as somehow queer (as paradoxical stereotypes of the asexual or oversexual person with disabilities would suggest), while queers are often understood as somehow disabled (as an ongoing medicalization of identity, similar to what people with disabilities more generally encounter would suggest). (McRuer 2006a: 94)

Roets, Adams and Van Hove (2006) tell a story which explains the potential danger of violence for disabled people falling outside the normative imagination of gender intelligibility. One of the authors, Marie Adams, has the label of intellectual impairment. The authors tell of the battles she and her allies faced when sterilisation was, in 2002, 'imposed on Marie as an absolute, ineluctable necessity' (Roets, Adams and Hove 2006: 167). The article explains that there was no attempt to engage Marie in informed discussions of sex and sexuality. Rather, people tried to scare her into agreeing to sterilisation; she was told that 'by going ahead with the sterilization she was never going to have trouble with "shady blokes who want to rape you" any more' (Roets et al. 2006: 170). With support from her self-advocacy group, mother and academic advocates, Marie resisted sterilisation. However the sterilisation of disabled young women is not only a historical phenomenon (Roets et al. 2006). Marie's fight took place in Belgium in 2002. Furthermore, although the occurrence of surgical sterilisation may have decreased, young women with the label of intellectual impairment are often given long-term contraception, without explanation, their knowledge or consent (Chamberlain, Rauh, Passer, McGrath and Burket 1984; McCarthy 1998; Tilley, Walmsley, Earle and Atkinson 2012). The justification often used is that sterilisation/long-term contraception prevents abuse (McCarthy 1998). Such arguments not only remove blame from violent perpetrators and place responsibility upon women, but *increase* the likelihood of abuse, as much abuse is perpetuated by male family and staff members, who presumably realise their persecution is reduced as detection through pregnancy will not occur (McCarthy 1998: 571).

Marie's story also alerts us to links between disability, non-normative sexuality *and* a child-like state of being. Declared 'sexually unfit', Marie is also deemed incapable of making other decisions that we may associate with adulthood, such as controlling her own finances. To think about this further, I want think more about the relationship between youth and sexuality, by reintroducing the border zone of youth (Lesko 2012).

The Policing of Genders at the Border Zone of Youth

In Chapter 2 youth as border zone revealed youth to us, not as a rationalised, scientific 'truth', but a 'social fact'; produced through disciplining technologies which aim to put young people on the 'correct' tracks to adulthood

(Lesko 2002). The border zone is reliant upon ableist discourses of development: scientific and psychological beliefs that by a certain *age* one should be at a certain *stage* (Burman 2008; Goodley and Runswick-Cole 2010; Slater 2013). Technologies such as schools, families and youth services work to shape the incomplete, irrational, unproductive, asexual child into the complete, rational, productive, and (crucial for this chapter), *sexual,* adult. With youth comes the expectation of a developing sexuality. These stages therefore also vary dependent upon normatively gendered expectations (Burman 2008). These expectations rest upon both developmental assumptions, and an assumption of the sexual innocence of children. Yet, in reality, lessons as to what count as ab/normal genders and sexuality start early; even if not explicitly delivered through formal education, they are taught through the media, peers, and the mundane conversations with family, teachers and so on (Evans 2002; Robinson 2008). Cavanagh (2010) argues that training toddlers to use the toilet, is also 'gender training'. Parenting manuals, for example, encourage mothers to 'toilet train' their daughters, whilst fathers pay attention to their sons. From this point onwards, we must choose either 'male' or 'female' when we use the toilet, and gender binaries are therefore confirmed through the most mundane of acts. Similarly, Davies (2003) highlights the implicit ways children 'learn' what it is to be a boy/girl through toys, clothing and different behaviours being deemed 'appropriate'. Furthermore, Evans (2002) highlights that whilst conversations about queer relationships are always noticed (if not taboo) in the classroom, those of heterosexual relationships both are rife and implicit (see also Chapman 2013).

As children grow older and reach 'youth', talk around gender often shifts to more explicit conversations about sexuality. Yet, the messages delivered are far from clear. On the one hand, we have already seen, the youthful body 'sells' (Slater 2012). Young people are exposed to highly sexualised images of their peers, and taught about the implicit culturally-embedded relationships between youth and the body beautiful. Yet, there is another, juxtaposing, side to the coin: young people are paradoxically also 'subject to the requirements of proper dress and discipline' (Wyn and White 2000: 165); and these 'requirements' are gendered (Lesko 2012). The 'uniforms' – both explicit in the sense of school uniform, and implicit, in the sense of meeting cultural expectation – are different for girls and young women, than they are for boys and young men. Furthermore, an often implicit 'boys will be boys' discourse teaches young men they are 'expected to be aggressive sexual actors attempting to 'get' sex from passive women who both hold and embody sex itself' (Filipovic 2008: 19). Importantly for us, and as McRuer's (2006a, 2006b) analysis hints at, the expectations also vary dependent upon perception of dis/ability. If we think back to Cavanagh's (2010) toilets, for example, we realise that the accessible (or 'disabled') toilet is usually gender neutral. If toilet training is gender training, what does that teach disabled people about their genders and sexualities (see Kafer 2011, for a good discussion of this)? This quote from a participatory study with young disabled people around sex education at school exemplifies some of these complexities well:

> In a discussion about sex education at school, the one group member who had attended a mainstream school said they had been shown videos of very difficult births in order to scare girls off having sex and getting pregnant. Those who had attended special schools were amazed at this. In special schools, they said, teachers 'would have been too frightened to talk about sex or relationships'. One of the young women in the group had strong views on this issue. She said it was typical of the way special schools treated students that it simply would not occur to them that a girl with a disability might get pregnant before leaving school.

> 'They couldn't let you do that [talk about having sex] because the cotton wool would be broken. The cotton wool that they wrap you up in the day you start. By the time you leave the cotton wool has pretty much smothered you'. (Horgan 2003: 104–5)

In the 'special school' disabled young people were presumed passive; incapable of having sex and getting pregnant, so they were told nothing. In the 'mainstream school', however, young people were considered dangerously active: sex and pregnancy was considered a risk. To scare them from both practices, they were taught that having sex and getting pregnant are bad and painful experiences (S. Duncan, Edwards and Alexander 2010). Neither scenario is helpful; both are disciplining practices aiming to shape a certain type of person (Foucault 1977); and arguably part of larger cultures of violence (Friedman and Valenti 2008). Nowhere is it acknowledged that teenagers can and do make good parents (S. Duncan et al. 2010). Young people are not taught that sex should be fun and pleasurable (Friedman and Valenti 2008). There is no attempt to expand notions of sex and sexuality outside of sex being about penis-in-vagina intercourse that leads to babies (a bad thing) (S. Duncan et al. 2010). Rather, biopolitical regimes mean that we see the infantilisation of those considered passive and attempts are also made to pacify those who are considered 'active' through misinformation, scaremongering and demonisation.

This presumption of asexuality and passivity became apparent in the stories of young disabled women I met while I was running a workshop with a youth forum of a disabled people's campaigning organisation in the UK. In the break, Molly, a 21-year-old disabled woman with a physical impairment, told me a tale of her 16-year-old self. Molly used to be a swimmer and wanted to start taking the pill so her periods would be predictable and not get in the way of her swimming. She went to the doctor, who was happy to gratify her request.

However, when running through his list of questions he became embarrassed; his phrasing going something as follows:

> Erm ... I'm really sorry but I've, erm, got to ask you this ... and I know, well, of course you're not, I mean, I know you're not, but I do have to ask, you're not sexually active ... are you?

The confused and anxiety-causing rhetoric which surrounds disability and sexuality emerges as an assumption of asexuality (Mollow 2012; Shildrick 2009). Although Molly laughed as she told this story, she deemed it a 'laugh or cry' situation. The ableist relationships between disability, youth, gender and sexuality posit young disabled people outside of adultist gender intelligibility. They are assumed to be asexual and, as such, this prevents them crossing the border zone of youth (Garland-Thomson 2002; Liddiard 2012). Though this positioning, they are also positioned as childlike (Baron, Riddell and Wilson 1999).

We see the importance, then, of shifting the relationship between disability, gender and sexuality away from one of perceived abnormality by exploring the violent cultures within which they are perpetuated. Butler (Butler 1993a, 1999) and McRuer (2006b) give us space to think about the possibilities of resistance. Butler claims that the heterosexual ideal is only solidified through performativity, and McRuer (2006a, 2006b) argues that the ideal able-bodied identity is similarly performative. Whilst Butler has 'gender trouble', therefore, McRuer has 'ability trouble'. For both Butler and McRuer, considering gender and/or dis/ability as performative also reveals space to subvert these normative roles (Sandahl 1999). They both make the importance of this clear, arguing that simply recognising discourses of gender and dis/ability as socially and culturally constituted will not necessarily lead to their un-doing . They therefore ask us to 'work to the weakness in the norm' (McRuer 2006b: 30). For Butler (1993b) this means being 'critically queer'; and for McRuer (2006b) it means being 'severely disabled': using the inevitable failure to meet up to the heterosexual/able-bodied 'ideal' as a way of mobilising. I consider this further now by turning to tell another of the many stories of young disabled people resisting their societal positioning from my fieldwork.

Resistance

I captured the following story in my research diary after going downtown with Freyja and Embla (who are more fully introduced in Chapter 4) on my first Saturday night in Reykjavik:

Embla arrives to pick me up so I rush out. Freyja's going to meet us later, Embla tells me: she still needs to do her makeup. She takes *ages* doing her make-up, so will probably be late. I turn to look at Embla: she's wearing a black dress, leather jacket, heeled boots, face made-up, and hair done. Nothing unusual there, she always looks great. I catch a glimpse of myself in the rear-view mirror: make-up-less, hair a mess. I look down at my attire: the usual jeans, my most 'Icelandic' woolly jumper, hidden under my raincoat. Gloves, hat and snow-boots finish the outfit off nicely. Mum would be pleased at least: very sensible clothing for the cold weather. Maybe I won't feel so comfortable with the hipsters of trendy downtown Reykjavik though. 'You look nice', I say to Embla, 'I'm going to feel a right scruff coming out with you two'. 'Don't worry about it', Embla reassures me, 'it's okay for you. You're not disabled. I have to get dressed up; I don't want to live the disability stereotype!'(Research diary, 4th February 2012)

Embla, Freyja and I had many conversations around this whilst I was in Iceland. As Mingus (2011) suggests, these conversations became 'difficult', as discussions of dressing our bodies could not stop at or be separated from the myriad of societal positionings we experienced through our embodied identities. The three of us are all white, cis gendered, young women in our early-to-mid-20s. None of us are immigrants or poor, and we are all involved to different degrees in the middle-class world of academia, particularly disability studies and the social sciences. Embla and myself both identify as queer, Embla as lesbian, whilst Freyja identifies as straight. Freyja and Embla, unlike myself, are disabled women with visible, physical impairments. The ways we experienced the identities we had in common (and the ways we felt able to challenge our societal positionings based on these) were therefore different. The expectation on me as a non-disabled young woman that night was to dress up, and conform to the dress code of most other young women out. Freyja and Embla therefore felt that through my non-disabled embodiment, I was able to trouble the commodification and objectification of women's bodies by making a decision to not put on make-up and get dressed up on a night out. Yet, they described how, as disabled women, their troubling had to work differently. Despite what Embla called a feminist impulse to challenge the objectification of women's bodies, my disabled friends felt it was more important to assert themselves as gendered and sexual beings. This meant asserting a femme[4] identity.

---

4   Whereas I defined femininity earlier as an ideological system, femme has been defined as 'someone who consciously chooses to embrace fem(me)ininity as a "deviant" identity [...] The major difference between a feminine woman and a femme is conscious gender performance, and anyone who consciously takes on the role of femininity as a deviant identity can be femme' (Femme Galaxy 2011).

Taking the 'not bothering' option would (as Embla puts it) mean 'living the stereotype of the cute little disabled girl'.

Some of these complexities are discussed by Smith (2014) and Ndopu (2013). Both are (visibly) disabled people, bloggers, activists and academics with an interest in fashion. Both mark clothing as a site to challenge stereotypes of disabled people as 'a pitiful, unattractive, sexless homogeneous mass' (Smith 2014). Ndopu explains that wearing trendy, fashionable clothes means they are read differently than when wearing casual clothes, writing that '[o]ver time, I realized that non-disabled folks re-inscribed my casual attire with a social meaning that rendered my body the personification of dishevelment and neglect'. Furthermore, appreciating the complexities of identity, Ndopu goes go on to note that the 'representation of Crips as the objects of deprivation and targets of charity [...] is made all the more stark by the fact that I am a Black Queer Crip of the African diaspora' (Ndopu 2013). Similarly to Ndopu's (2013) analysis, Freyja and Embla's argument was that if they chose to not wear make-up and 'dress up' on a night out, they wouldn't be considered a challenge to the feminine ideal, but 'objects of deprivation and targets of charity' (Ndopu 2013). Thus, their approach was to fight for their acceptance within consumer culture; a move Garland-Thompson (2002) (in a discussion of disabled fashion models) terms 'inadvertent activism'.

However, Embla also told me that although 'dressing up' is a conscious political decision, she felt unable to take the 'not bothering' option, even when she couldn't 'be bothered'. Although the way we present ourselves can be a conscious act of resistance, this resistance is functioning within larger systemic constraints, which deem our bodies a locus of social control (Ndopu 2013). In Foucauldian terms, biopolitical systems regulate the ways in which resistance to homogenising discourses can play out. Ndopu deems such a constraint 'the confines of the able normative imagination':

> I've come to realize that very often, for the sake of our survival, we must subscribe to hegemonic standards of ontology and desirability because those standards have social currency that in some cases lessen the threat of violence and in other cases improve economic conditions. (Ndopu 2013)

We see that, for disabled young women (and others who fall outside of the normative imagination of gender intelligibility), making a safe crossing to adulthood is about survival, and not without sacrifice (see Chapter 3). It is perhaps because of this urge for survival that some disability studies scholars have argued the normativity of young disabled people's sexuality. Morris (2002: 7), for example, writes that 'sex and sexuality figure as important issues in the transition to adulthood for non-disabled young people but adults do not always recognise that disabled young people will have the same sexual feelings of others of their age'. It is arguably thanks to an argument that disabled people are 'just like everybody else' that there has been a degree of liberal acceptance (see Chapter 1) around *some* disabled people's sexual presence. Yet, as asserted throughout this book, stopping at such an analysis can be dangerous (Sothern 2007). It is, as Mingus (2011) would say, an 'easy(ish) conversation' that fails to tackle wider and intersectional cultures of violence. Many of those arguing the normalisation of disabled people's sexuality do it through presuming a biological 'naturalness' of heterosexuality (Brown 1994). Thus, although this may assist some disabled young people in crossing the border zone of youth, for others it means remaining an unintelligible subject. Kim (2011: 479), for example, points out that the stereotype of disabled people's asexuality has largely been resisted by perpetuating the normative assumption of a 'universal presence of sexual desire'. She questions the place in such a movement for a disabled person who doesn't experience their sexuality in this way, someone for example, who may *identify* as asexual. Furthermore, both Sothern (2007) and Löfgren-Mårtenson (2013) highlight that the concern for disabled people's sexualities (particularly those with learning difficulties) to be considered within 'the norm' both maintains and relies upon dominant heterosexual ideologies of masculinity and femininity, leaving little space for explorations of gender and sexuality outside of a heterosexual matrix. When I was in Iceland I met a friend of Embla and Freyja's who was doing her BA research into attitudes towards disabled lesbians (Skjaldardóttir 2012). Her findings supported Sothern's concerns. Whilst doing this research she was not surprised to find that there was little support for disabled lesbians, she was, however, shocked at the response of many of her friends when she told them the subject of her research, who replied: '*disabled lesbians ... is there such a thing?*' I follow Sothern (2007: 151), therefore, when he writes that arguing that disabled people are 'just the same as everybody else' relies on 'reinforcing the binary construction of gender through which disabled bodies (and others) become Othered'.

Yet, there are other things going on in the story of going Downtown, and I do not wish to be too pessimistic here. On first reading, my own 'dressing down' and Embla's 'dressing up' could be presumed to be acting in opposition to, and perhaps un-doing the work of one-another. Whilst I could be perceived as challenging the objectification of women's bodies, Embla strives to be accepted within it. We are challenging each other's political projects. Yet, McRuer (2006a, 2006b) argues that like the heterosexual ideal, the performativity of ability has been normalised, naturalised, to the extent that it goes unnoticed. The normative expectation on me as a young non-disabled woman is to perform femininity. A performance of this femininity, however, would not emerge as an utterance, but a silence. In failing to perform femininity, however, attention is brought to my embodiment in a way a 'dressing up' may not have done. Embla's non-normative embodiment, on the other hand, becomes a spectacle (Shildrick 1997). For disabled young women, the expectation is not to cross into normative adulthood by meeting gendered and sexual norms, but to remain the genderless, asexual eternal child (Baron et al. 1999). By failing to perform 'ability', Embla inevitably fails in a performance of femininity and heterosexuality (McRuer 2006a). Therefore, through a performance of femme, her embodiment acts as resistance. Furthermore, Embla not only stands as a challenge to the discourse of disabled people as genderless and asexual (Liddiard 2011), but also destabilises the ableism inherent to gender norms associated with femininity (McRuer 2006a). As Mingus says, 'it's complicated …'.

A Politic of Ugliness?

What would it mean then, to have a politic of ugliness? To, as Mingus (2011) asks us, shift conversations 'from [easy] conversations of beauty and easy and me, to [difficult conversations of] ugly and magnificence and we'? We have seen in the chapter complex entanglements of femininity, youth, sexuality, gender, disability and the body. Like previous discussions in this book, the conversations tell us of the potential dangers and difficulties of crossing the border zone of youth for those considered outside the norm; that easy conversations may, at times, be about survival. Mingus acknowledges this:

> And I am not saying it is easy to be ugly without apology. It is hard as fuck. It threatens our survival. I recognize the brilliance in our instinct to move toward beauty and desirability. And it takes time and for some of us it may be impossible. I know it is complicated … And I also know that though it may be a way to survive, it will not be a way to thrive, to grow the kind of genders and world we need. And it is not attainable to everyone, even those who want it to be. (Mingus 2011)

None of the ideas that we've talked about in this chapter (nor the book) give us a blueprint to what a 'difficult conversation' around bodies, youth, sexuality, dis/ability and so on would look/sound like. They do, however, make us realise the importance of paying attention to the multiple axes of identity which we all inhabit (Crenshaw 1989), and realising that what we are able to do, including the ways we are able to resist, will change from time and place, depending on our relative positionings of privilege and marginalisation (Pillow 2003).

In fact, what they perhaps make us realise is that the conversations need to be multiple. Although sometimes the conversations may play out differently, with different people, at different times, spaces are needed to bring them together and think them next to one-another (Kafer 2013). Sothern (2007: 147) argues that in (neo)liberal societies, rather than seeing an explicit segregation and overt intolerability of difference, we see instead see a 'liberal intolerability of difference', which manifests itself in different ways. This is the tyranny of Mr Reasonable. In order to be rendered 'knowable', both queer sexualities and the disabled body have to be rendered 'normal'. Once 'normal' they are accepted within a certain 'knowable', 'normal' framework which 'puts pressure on disabled bodies to be sexualised in hegemonically knowable ways' (Sothern 2007: 152). For some, however, this will remain unattainable. The next and final chapter is the one in which we wave goodbye to Mr Reasonable as I outline some more academic/activist/pedagogical ideas for moving forward.

Chapter 7
The Limits of 'Sameness': Goodbye Mr Reasonable

The concept of 'intersectionality' can be read [...] as a call to watching our watching, to reading our readings, and to uncover a few of the ways we identify differences, including those differences that are today identified as disability.

(Titchkosky 2007: 3)

An overarching aim of this book, following Crenshaw (1989) and other black feminist scholars (e.g. Guinier 1994; hooks 1982; Lorde 2012), has been to intersectionally explore how multiple forms of oppression co-constitute one-another at the border zone of youth (Lesko 2012). I have done this with a focus on disability, a devalued form of difference that is often left aside in otherwise important intersectional conversations (Erevelles 2011; Titchkosky 2007). An eye on the 'reasonableness' of 'adulthood', however, has meant that although these stories started with disability, they have never ended with it (Goodley 2011). I have argued that the systemic conditions of ableism, entwined with norms of white supremacy, heteropatriarchy, and global capitalism (Chapters 2, 3 and 6), allow for violent acts of disablism to be rendered reasonable. Furthermore, the reasonableness of this oppression, leads to a dyad which dangerously renders some people as reasonable, whilst others are deemed unreasonable (Chapter 3 and 5).

The point of this book then has been unpick disabled young people's stories and negotiations of un/reasonableness at the border zone of youth (Lesko 2012). This has required us, as Titchkosky (2007: 3) puts it, to 'watch our watching' and 'read our readings'. Exploring how a dangerous discourse of reasonableness manifests itself at the intersection of youth and disability, I have argued that an often well intentioned liberal plea for 'sameness' (Chapter 1) is not just insufficient, but dangerously in compliance with values of reasonable exclusion. By a liberal plea for sameness, I mean a call that disabled young people are no different from anybody else – i.e. that they are becoming-adult just like their non-disabled peers (Chapter 2). I have made it clear in this book, however, that my problem with this argument is not one of disabled young people's sameness, difference or otherwise. Rather, my problem with the argument is a lack of interrogation into who exactly is this 'everybody else'. My argument has been that this everybody else is representative of the failures of the normative imagination; the Mr Reasonable who has been haunting this book. Therefore, although a call for sameness may appear (or intend to be) 'liberating', it in fact plays into the hands of individualising, (neo)liberal doctrine. Calling for 'sameness' means if some people don't fare well once we're all rendered 'the same', the failure becomes not one of systems, but one of individual deficit, meaning their 'exclusion from culture is more justified than ever' (Ferguson and Ferguson 2001: 84). As Barton put it (1993: 241), the only 'equality' evoked is the 'equality of opportunity to become unequal'.

To become 'the same', to reach the desired adulthood of Mr Reasonable, is to fit into the very systems that serve to oppress us (Sothern 2007). Moreover, we have seen through this book that the pressure to be 'the same' weighs down most heavily on those marginalised through this very discourse. Young disabled people in Chapter 3, for example, told us that they had to go above and beyond their non-disabled peers in proving themselves 'reasonably adult'. This left them little time to rest from their fight for adulthood acceptance; little time to 'be young' (in whatever forms this may take). Additionally, proving 'sameness' often meant that young disabled people had to distance themselves from other forms of Otherness. Freyja, for example, made disabled people's right to hire their own assistants recognisable as 'reasonable', by buying into gendered norms and consumerist discourse (Chapter 3). Far from coalition, an argument striving for acceptance through sameness can lead to further marginalisation of those who do not/cannot/will not conform. The ways to become are increasingly restricted.

Yet, despite the doom and gloom, there have also been many stories of young people's resistance to paths laid out shared within this book. Chapter 4, for instance, told of the ways in which some young disabled people I spent time with were involved in the wider struggles of disabled people's movements. Learning from redefinitions of 'independence' provided by the Independent Living Movement, and feminist conversations of relational autonomy, helped me to interrogate the normative developmental presumption of a shift from childhood dependency to adulthood independency. Perhaps here I did touch upon a narrative of 'sameness'. However, rather than argue disabled young people are the same as everybody else in their youth-adult trajectories, I followed Greenstein and Graby (2013) in considering autonomy, not as a destination, something any one of us does or does not *have*, but as always something relational that we struggle together towards. None of us, we saw, can embody independent adulthood. Mr Reasonable's claims of adulthood seem increasingly farcical as we consider youth not as about becoming-adult, but as part of a continual becoming of life.

Struggle and conflict didn't only happen within these overt activist battles, however. We also saw the subversion of paths laid out happening in more mundane spaces (Chapter 5). I emphasise the importance of recognising and celebrating acts of resistance and subversion (of which we've seen many) however small these may appear. At the same time, however, we need to appreciate and challenge the structures which allow for the conditions this subversion happens within (Erevelles 2011). Chapters 3, 5 and 6 all helped us to see how the ways in which resistance plays out is dependent upon larger systemic constraints (Ndopu 2013). As important as they are to tell, individual stories must therefore always be set within their socio-cultural-political context (Curran and Runswick-Cole 2013).

This book, of course, has offered only partial readings, and should only ever be read as such. It is a construction, written by me (with the help of others) at a particular moment in time. Switching my laptop off late last night, I poured a glass of red wine, and ran a bath. As I lay amongst the bubbles and sipped my wine I re-read the introductory chapter to Erevelles (2011) book, *Disability and Difference in Global Context*. Already I wanted to pull my own book apart and do it again differently. Positionality is always particular to a moment in time. There are already parts of this book that frustrate me, and on each reading, I will probably come across other parts I find frustrating. You have probably made different analyses to me, or noticed things missing that I haven't (yet). The book is, for example, very much located in the Global North. Experiences of race have been theorised, but due to the conversations and identities of the young disabled people with whom I spent time, they have been peripheral to, rather than a core part of the analysis. As well as theorising around the exclusion of some spaces we may consider to be part of 'youth culture' in Chapter 5, it would have been interesting to think more about youth subcultures that may claim allegience with disabilty (the freak spectacle? Geek cultures?); and to think how/if technology has altered the changing relationships between disabled young people and youth culture. Furthermore, it became particularly apparent when writing Chapter 6, that there has been a lack of engagement with disabled young people who identify as trans*. I see this book, however, not as an end, but a provocative springboard for new beginnings. Nevertheless, the following have been particularly important to my still developing critique of disablitiy at the border zone of youth:

1. Avoiding liberal arguments based on 'sameness' and remain vigilant to discourses of 'reasonableness' (reasonableness only ever functions to marginalise).

2. Questioning, in any argument, what norms are being bought into, and who is being marginalised by these norms ('watch your watching', Titchkosky 2007: 3).

3. Drawing on and learning from those writing and acting in other disciplines and movements – critical race theory, queer theory, and feminist movements, particularly black feminism and feminist theory coming from the global south (the latter is something I need to engage with more).

4. Treating theory as a resource (Hughes, Goodley and Davis 2012), a way to navigate the world, or indeed as healing (hooks 1994), rather than a hierarchical system that only some people should have access to (blogs have taught me a lot).

5. Considering mundane acts of oppression (disablism, racism, sexism, homo/transphobia etc.) as part of larger cultures of structural violence.

6. Appreciating ableism as always intersectional and tied in with heteropatriarchy, white supremacy and global capitalism (don't avoid 'difficult conversations' around this, Mingus 2010).

The above have become part of this book to differing degrees. Equally important, however, as I hope I've made a case for through this book, is to note that disability needs to be explored as a political identity alongside race, sexuality, class, gender and so on, in *any* theorisation which involves disabled people (and this will most likely be any theorisation which involves *people*). Researching for this book has illuminated many occasions where this hasn't been the case (Chapters 2, 5 and 6).

I end the book here, like I began. Remembering that bits of Mr Reasonable are harboured in all of us, I close with a word to Mr Reasonable (me? You?).

Dear Mr Reasonable,

As we've already come a long way together, this is just a quick note; it'd be rude to leave without saying goodbye. I was wondering what you've learnt through our discussions in this book? I'm hoping that you're clearer now as to why, in the first letter I sent you, I deemed you the creation of systems. We've seen that discourses of (neo)liberal adulthood serve to benefit those already in power (Chapter 1). These are people, like you, who manage to 'play grownup' (Slater 2013) better than others. We've exposed the 'adulthood' you hold so close to your heart as a façade, built on racist, ableist, patriarchal and heteronormative systems. Not being accepted as 'adult' is therefore not individual failure or deficit, but the prejudice of developmental discourse (Chapter 2). Yet it nevertheless has consequences. Do you get now, that your cries to '*be reasonable, we have to draw the line somewhere*' (Titchkosky 2012) make you the guardian of these oppressive systems (Chapter 3)? I'm asking you now then, to pause next time before you cry for 'reason'; before you tell another they're being 'unreasonable'. 'Watch your watching' and 'read your readings' (Titchkosky 2007: 3), struggle together with those around you (Chapter 4), and notice who is not present in the spaces you exist within. Moreover, challenge the reasonableness of this exclusion (Chapter 5).

We've seen through this book that resistance isn't easy. It will play out differently between individuals, dependent upon time and place (Chapter 6). You may need to relinquish some of your power; listening, rather than always being the first one to speak. It will certainly require 'difficult conversations' (Mingus 2011), both with others and with yourself. These conversations probably won't have straightforward answers. The point is, however, to think more critically about what is implicitly considered reasonable, and to whom this reasonable rhetoric is doing harm. The overall message for you, Mr Reasonable, is this: next time you feel yourself slipping into what may be oppressive to others, don't play into systems that render their oppression reasonable. Rather, stop playing grownup.

Love from,

Jen x

References

Adams, T.E. and Holman Jones, S. (2011). Telling Stories: Reflexivity, Queer Theory, and Autoethnography. *Cultural Studies ↔ Critical Methodologies*, 11(2), 108–16.

ALLFIE. (2012). *The Alliance for Inclusive Education – Our Position on Academies and Free Schools*. Retrieved from ALLFIE http://www.allfie.org.uk/docs/Academies%20 Position%20FINAL%20Dec%202012.doc (accessed 8 October 2013).

Askheim, O.P. (2003). Personal Assistance for People with Intellectual Impairments: Experiences and Dilemmas. *Disability & Society*, 18(3), 325–39.

Atkins, D. (ed.) (1998). *Looking Queer: Body Image and Identity in Lesbian, Bisexual, Gay and Transgender Communities*. New York and London: Harrington Park Press.

Atkinson, P. and Hammersley, M. (1994). Ethnography and Participant Observation. In N.K. Denzin and Y.S. Lincoln (eds), *Handbook of Qualitative Research*. London and New Delhi: Sage Publications, 248–61.

Bailey, S. (2011, 10th August). Riots without Responsibility, Comment. *The Guardian*. Retrieved from http://www.guardian.co.uk/commentisfree/2011/ aug/10/riots-without-responsibility (accessed 10 November 2014).

Barber, B.R. (2007). *Consumed: How Markets Corrupt Children, Infantilize Adults, and Swallow Citizens Whole*. New York: W.W. Norton & Company.

Barnes, C. (1992). Disabling Imagery and the Media. An Exploration of the Principles for Media Representations of Disabled People. Retrieved from Leeds Disability Archive, http://www.leeds.ac.uk/disability-studies/ archiveuk/Barnes/disabling%20imagery.pdf (accessed 22 November 2009).

Barnes, C. (2002). 'Emancipatory Disability Research': Project or Process. *Journal of Research in Special Educational Needs*, 2(1), 1–8.

Barnes, C. and Mercer, G. (1997). Breaking the Mould? An Introduction to Doing Disability Research. In C. Barnes (ed.), *Doing Disability Research*. Leeds: The Disability Press, 1, 1–14.

Baron, S., Riddell, S. and Wilson, A. (1999). The Secret of Eternal Youth: Identity, Risk and Learning Difficulties. *British Journal of Sociology of Education*, 20(4), 483–99.

Barton, L. (1993). The Struggle for Citizenship: The Case of Disabled People. *Disability & Society*, 8(3), 235–48.

BBC News. (2011). Disabled People Fear Housing Benefit Changes. London: BBC.

Beresford, P. (2002). Thinking about 'Mental Health': Towards a Social Model. *Journal of Mental Health*, 11(6), 581–84.

Bergman, S.B. (2009). Part-Time Fatso. In E. Rothblum and S. Soloway (eds), *The Fat Studies Reader*. New York and London: New York University Press, 139–42.

Berk, L.E. (2010). *Development Through the Lifespan* (5th edn). Boston: Pearson Education.

Biggs, S. and Powell, J.L. (2001). A Foucauldian Analysis of Old Age and the Power of Social Welfare. *Journal of Aging & Social Policy*, 12(2), 93–112.

Boero, N. (2009). Fat Kids, Working Moms, and the 'Epidemic of Obesity': Race, Class and Mother Blame. In E. Rothblum and S. Soloway (eds), *The Fat Studies Reader*. New York and London: New York University Press, 113–19.

Boffey, D. (2011, 15th May). Disabled People Face Abuse and Threats of Violence after Fraud Crackdown. *The Observer*. Retrieved from http://www.guardian.co.uk/society/2011/may/15/disability-living-allowance-scope-cuts (accessed 17 May 2011).

Bogdan, R. and Taylor, S.J. (1998). The Social Construction of Humanness: Relationships with People with Severe Retardation. In R. Bogdan and S.J. Taylor (eds), *Introduction to Qualitative Research Methods: A Guidebook and Resource* (3rd edn). Chichester: John Wiley & Sons, Inc., 242–58.

Bordo, S. (1993). *Unbearable Weight, Feminism, Western Culture and the Body*. Berkeley: University of California Press.

Boxall, K., Carson, I. and Docherty, D. (2004). Room at the Academy? People with Learning Difficulties and Higher Education. *Disability & Society*, 19(2), 99–112.

Bracking, R. and Cowan, S. (1998). *It's MY Life – An Introduction to Independent Living*. Retrieved from http://www.independentliving.org/docs4/bracking1.html (accessed 24 April 2014).

Brand, R. (2011, 12th August). Big Brother isn't Watching You. *The Guardian*, p. 4. Retrieved from http://www.guardian.co.uk/uk/2011/aug/11/london-riots-davidcameron (accessed 10 November 2014).

Brisenden, S. (1986). Independent Living and the Medical Model of Disability. *Disability, Handicap & Society*, 1(2), 173–8.

Brooks, M. (2006). Man-to-Man. *Qualitative Inquiry*, 12(1), 185–207.

Brown, H. (1994). 'An Ordinary Sexual Life?': A Review of the Normalisation Principle as It Applies to the Sexual Options of People with Learning Disabilities. *Disability and Society*, 9(2), 123–44.

Burman, E. (2008a). *Deconstructing Developmental Psychology*. Hove: Routledge.

Burman, E. (2008b). *Developments: Child, Image, Nation*. Hove: Routledge.

Butler, J. (1993a). *Bodies That Matter: On the Discursive Limits of "Sex"*. London: Routledge.

Butler, J. (1993b). Critically Queer. In *Bodies That Matter*. London: Routledge, 223–42.

Butler, J. (1999). *Gender Trouble: Feminism and the Subversion of Identity* (10th Anniversary edn). New York and London: Routledge.

Butler, P. (2011, 30th March). As the New Financial Year Kicks Off, Here's What We Know So Far. *The Guardian*, 2–3.

Butler, P. (2012a, 26 June). Disability Cuts: 'Thousands of Us Will become Prisoners in Our Own Homes'. *The Guardian*. Retrieved from http://www.guardian.co.uk/global/patrick-butler-cuts-blog/2012/jun/26/disability-benefit-cuts-will-damage-motability-car-undustry (accessed 13 October 2012).

Butler, P. (2012b, 22nd June). Disabled People Hit Especially Hard by Cuts, Finds Report. *The Guardian*. Retrieved from http://www.guardian.co.uk/society/2012/jun/22/disabled-people-hit-hard-cuts (accessed 13 October 2012).

Butler, R. (1998). Rehabilitating the Images of Disabled Youth. In T. Skelton and G. Valentine (eds), *Cool Places: Geographies of Youth Cultures*. London: Routledge, 83–100.

Calderbank, R. (2000). Abuse and Disabled People: Vulnerability or Social Indifference? *Disability & Society*, 15(3), 521–34.

Cameron, D. (2010, 19th July). *Big Society Speech*. Retrieved from https://www.gov.uk/government/speeches/big-society-speech (accessed 8 October 2012).

Campbell, F.K. (2009). *Contours of Ableism: The Production of Disability and Abledness*. Basingstoke: Palgrave Macmillan.

Campbell, F.K. (2012). Stalking Ableism: Using Disability to Expose 'Abled' Narcissism. In D. Goodley, B. Hughes and L. Davis (eds), *Disability and Social Theory: New Approaches and Directions*. Basingstoke and New York: Palgrave Macmillan, 212–30.

Carlson, L. and Kittay, E.F. (2010). Introduction: Rethinking Philosophical Presumptions in Light of Cognitative Disability. In E.F. Kittay and L. Carlson (eds), *Cognitive Disability and its Challenge to Moral Philosophy*. Oxford: Wiley-Blackwell, 1–26.

Cavanagh, A. and Dennis, A. (2012). Framing the Riots. *Capital & Class*, 36(3), 375–81.

Cavanagh, S.L. (2010). *Queering Bathrooms: Gender, Sexuality, and the Hygienic Imagination*. Toronto: University of Toronto Press.

Cave, T. (2013). Lessons to be Learned from Winterbourne View. *Nursing & Residential Care*, 15(1), 53–5.

Chamberlain, A., Rauh, J., Passer, A., McGrath, M. and Burket, R. (1984). Issues in Fertility Control for Mentally Retarded Female Adolescents: I. Sexual Activity, Sexual Abuse, and Contraception. *Pediatrics*, 73(4), 445–50.

Chandler, E. (2010). Sidewalk Stories: The Troubling Task of Identification. *Disability Studies Quarterly*, 30(3/4). Retrieved from http://www.dsq-sds.org/article/view/1293/1329 (accessed 17 November 2011).

Chapman, E.L. (2013). No More Controversial than a Gardening Display? Provision of LGBT-Related Fiction to Children and Young People in U.K. Public Libraries. *Library Trends*, 61(3), 542–68.

CILIP. (2012). Use of Volunteers: Full Policy Statement. Retrieved from http://www.cilip.org.uk/cilip/advocacy-awards-and-projects/advocacy-and-campaigns/public-libraries/policy-statements/use (accessed 14 October 2013).

Clarke, L.H. and Griffin, M. (2008). Visible and Invisible Ageing: Beauty Work as a Response to Ageism. *Ageing & Society*, 28(5), 653–74.

Code, L. (2000). The Perversion of Autonomy and the Subjection of Women: Discourses of Social Advocacy at Century's End. In C. Mackenzie and N. Stoljar (eds), *Relational Autonomy: Feminist Perspectives on Autonomy, Agency, and the Social Self*. New York: Oxford University Press, 181–213.

Collins, M. (2011). *Don't Forget the 'T' in LGBT*. Retrieved from http://www.diversitybestpractices.com/news-articles/dont-forget-t-lgbt (accessed 2 September 2014).

Corrigan, P. (2006). Doing Nothing. In S. Hall and T. Jefferson (eds), *Resistance through Rituals: Youth Subcultures in Post-war Britain* (2nd edn). Oxon and New York: Routledge, 84–7.

Crenshaw, K. (1989). Demarginalizing the Intersection of Race and Sex: A Black Feminist Critique of Antidiscrimination Doctrince, Feminist Theory and Antiracist Politics. *The University of Chicago Legal Forum*, 139–67.

Crow, L. (2012). Including All of Our Lives: Renewing the Social Model of Disability. In J. Rix, M. Nind, K. Sheehy, K. Simmons and C. Walsh (eds), *Equality, Participation and Inclusion 1: Diverse Perspectives* (2nd edn). Abingdon and New York: Routledge, 124–40.

Crowe, M. (2000). Constructing Normality: A Discourse Analysis of the DSM-IV. *Journal of Psychiatric and Mental Health Nursing*, 7(1), 69–77.

Curran, T. and Runswick-Cole, K. (eds) (2013). *Disabled Children's Childhood Studies: Critical Approaches in a Global Context*. Basingstoke: Palgrave Macmillan.

Davies, B. (2003). *Frogs and Snails and Feminist Tales: Preschool Children and Gender*. New York: Hampton Press.

Davis, L.J. (2001). Identity Politics, Disability, and Culture. In G.L. Albrecht, K.D. Seelman and M. Bury (eds), *Handbook of Disability Studies*. London: Sage Publications, Inc., 535–45.

Davis, L.J. (2002). *Bending over Backwards: Disability, Dismodernism, and Other Difficult Positions*. New York and London: New York University Press.

Davis, L.J. (2008). *Obsession: A History*. Chicago and London: The University of Chicago Press.

Davis, L.J. (2010). Constructing Normalcy. In L.J. Davis (ed.), *The Disability Studies Reader* (3rd edn). New York and London: Routledge, 3–19.

Deal, M. (2003). Disabled People's Attitudes toward Other Impairment Groups: A Hierarchy of Impairments. *Disability & Society*, 18(7), 897–910.

Deal, M. (2007). Aversive Disablism: Subtle Prejudice toward Disabled People. *Disability & Society*, 22(1), 93–107.

Denzin, N.K. (1998). The Art and Politics of Interpretation. In N.K. Denzin and Y.S. Lincoln (eds), *Collecting and Interpreting Qualitative Materials*. London: SAGE Publications, Ltd., 313–44.

Denzin, N.K. and Lincoln, Y.S. (1994). *Handbook of Qualitative Research*, edited by Norman K. Denzin and Yvonna S. Lincoln. Thousand Oaks, CA: Sage Publications.

Department for Education. (2013). Our Future – A Longitudinal Study of Young People in England. Retrieved from http://www.education.gov.uk/childrenandyoungpeople/youngpeople/ourfuture (accessed 22 August 2013).

Department of Works and Pensions. (2009). *Disability Living Allowance Claim for a Person aged 16 or Over*. London: HMSO.

DirectGov. (2011). Disabled People's Rights in Everyday Life. Retrieved from http://www.direct.gov.uk/en/disabledpeople/rightsandobligations/dg_4019061 (accessed 7 August 2012).

Dorn, N. and South, N. (1999). Youth, the Family and the Regulation of the 'Informal'. In N. South (ed.), *Youth Crime, Deviance and Delinquency* (vol. 1). Dartmouth: Ashgate.

Dowkey, A. (2004). The Treatment of Disability in 19th and Early 20th Century Children's Literature. *Disability Studies Quarterly*, 24(1). Retrieved from http://dsq-sds.org/article/view/843/1018 (accessed 10 November 2014).

Duncan, C. and Loretto, W. (2004). Never the Right Age? Gender and Age-Based Discrimination in Employment. *Gender, Work & Organization*, 11(1), 95–115.

Duncan, S., Edwards, R. and Alexander, C. (2010). *Teenage Parenthood: What's the Problem?* London: Tufnell.

Elliott, L. (2012, 8th March). George Osborne's Austerity Cuts will Hit Poorest Families Hardest, Experts Warn. *The Guardian*. Retrieved from http://www.guardian.co.uk/politics/2012/mar/08/george-osborne-austerity-cuts-poor-families (accessed 10 November 2014).

Ellis, C. (2007). Telling Secrets, Revealing Lives. *Qualitative Inquiry*, 13(1), 3–29.

Ellis, C. and Bochner, A.P. (2000). Autoethnography, Personal Narrative, Reflexivity. In N.K. Denzin and Y.S. Lincoln (eds), *Handbook of Qualitative Research* (2nd edn). London: Sage Publications, Inc., 733–68.

ENIL. (1992). *Definition of Independent Living*. Retrieved from http://www.independentliving.org/docs2/enildocs.html (accessed 10 December 2013).

Erevelles, N. (1996). Disability and the Dialectics of Difference. *Disability &* *Society*, 11(4), 519–38.

Erevelles, N. (2011). *Disability and Difference in Global Contexts*. New York: Palgrave Macmillan.

Etherington, K. (2007). Ethical Research in Reflexive Relationships. *Qualitative Inquiry*, 13(5), 599–616.

Evans, J. (2003). *The Independent Living Movement in the UK*. Retrieved from http://www.independentliving.org/docs6/evans2003.html#1 (accessed 18 December 2012).

Evans, K. (2002). *Negotiating the Self: Identity, Sexuality, and Emotion in Learning to Teach*. New York: Routledge Falmer.

Evans, S. (2004). *Forgotten Crimes: The Holocaust and People with Disabilities*. Chicago: Ivan R. Dee.

Every Disabled Child Matters. (2007). *Disabled Children and Child Poverty*. London: Every Disabled Child Matters.

Every Disabled Child Matters. (2011, 4th April). *Disabled Children's Benefits Cut by 50% under New Proposals*. Retrieved http://www.ncb.org.uk/edcm/news/news_archive/2011_news_archive/01_apr_11_la_duty/4_apr_11_premiums.aspx (accessed 20 December 2012).

Every Disabled Child Matters. (2012). *One in Seven Working Families with Disabled Children Going without Food*. Retrieved from http://www.edcm.org.uk/news/news-archive/2012/may-2012/counting-the-costs-2012.aspx (accessed 7 May 2012).

Facer, K. (2011a, 21st July). *Democracy, Education and Reclaiming Narratives of the Future*. Paper presented at the Summer Institute in Qualitative Research, Education and Social Research Institute, Manchester Metropolitan University.

Facer, K. (2011b). *Learning Futures: Education, Technology and Social Change*. Oxon: Routledge.

Facer, K. (2013). The Problem of the Future and the Possibilities of the Present in Education Research. *International Journal of Educational Research*, 61(0), 135–43.

Featherstone, M. (1982). The Body in Consumer Culture. *Theory, Culture &* *Society*, 1(2), 18–33.

Femme Galaxy. (2011). *Femme is ….* Retrieved from http://www.femmegalaxy.com/authors/tai-scarlet-kulystin/ (accessed 18 July 2014).

Ferguson, P.M. and Ferguson, D.L. (2001). Winks, Blinks, Squints and Twitches: Looking for Disability, Culture and Self-determination through Our Son's Left Eye. *Scandinavian Journal of Disability Research*, 3(2), 71–90.

Ferris, J. (2010). In (Disability) Time. *Disability Studies Quarterly*, 30(3/4). Retrieved from http://www.dsq-sds.org/article/view/1292/1328 (accessed 16 June 2011).

Filipovic, J. (2008). Offensive Feminism: The Conservative Gender Norms That Perpetuate Rape Culture, and How Feminists Can Fight Back. In J. Friedman and J. Valenti (eds), *Yes Means Yes!: Visions of Female Sexual Power and a World Without Rape*. Berkeley (CA): Seal Press, 13–28.

Fisanick, C. (2009). Fatness (In)visible: Polycystic Ovarian Syndrome and the Rhetoric of Normative Feminity. In E. Rothblum and S. Soloway (eds), *The Fat Studies Reader*. New York and London: New York University Press, 106–9.

Fitzgerald, H. and Kirk, D. (2009). Identity Work: Young Disabled People, Family and Sport. *Leisure Studies*, 28(4), 469–88.

Foucault, M. (1973). *The Birth of the Clinic: An Archaeology of Medical Perception*. London: Tavistock Publications Ltd.

Foucault, M. (1977). *Discipline and Punish – The Birth of the Prison* (A. Sheridan, trans.). New York: Pantheon Books.

Foucault, M. (1979). *History of Sexuality* (R. Hurley, trans., vol. 1). London: Allen Lane.

Friedman, J. and Valenti, J. (2008). *Yes Means Yes!: Visions of Female Sexual Power and a World Without Rape*. CA: Seal Press.

Fuller, T. and Loogma, K. (2009). Constructing Futures: A Social Constructionist Perspective on Foresight Methodology. *Futures*, 41(2), 71–9.

Galtung, J. (1990). Cultural Violence. *Journal of Peace Research*, 27(3), 291–305.

Garland-Thomson, R. (2002). Integrating Disability, Transforming Feminist Theory. *NWSA Journal*, 14(3), 1–32.

Garthwaite, K. (2011). 'The Language of Shirkers and Scroungers?' Talking about Illness, Disability and Coalition Welfare Reform. *Disability & Society*, 26(3), 369–72.

Geoghegan, V. (1987). *Utopianism and Marxism*. London: Methuen.

Gergen, K.J. (2008). *An Invitation to Social Construction* (2nd edn). London: SAGE.

Ghosh, P. (2013a, 14th May). Brain Scan Study to Understand Workings of Teenage Mind. *BBC News: Health*. Retrieved from http://www.bbc.co.uk/news/health-22510866 (accessed 20 August 2013).

Ghosh, P. (2013b). Brain Scan Study to Understand Workings of Teenage Mind. London: *BBC News*.

Gibson-Graham, J.K. (1999). Queer(y)ing Capitalism In and Out of the Classroom [1]. *Journal of Geography in Higher Education*, 23(1), 80–85.

Gibson, B.E. (2006). Disability, Connectivity and Transgressing the Autonomous Body. *Journal of Medical Humanities*, 27(3), 187–96.

Gibson, B.E., Brooks, D., DeMatteo, D. and King, A. (2009). Consumer-directed Personal Assistance and 'Care': Perspectives of Workers and Ventilator Users. *Disability & Society*, 24(3), 317–30.

Gibson, B.E., Carnevale, F.A. and King, G. (2012). 'This is My Way': Reimagining Disability, In/dependence and Interconnectedness of Persons and Assistive Technologies. *Disability & Rehabilitation, Early Online*, 1–6.

Giroux, H. (2009). *Youth in a Suspect Society: Democracy or Disposability?* New York: Palgrave Macmillan.

Goltz, D. (2009). Investigating Queer Future Meanings. *Qualitative Inquiry*, 15(3), 561–86.

Goodley, D. (1999). Disability Research and the 'Researcher Template': Reflections on Grounded Subjectivity in Ethnographic Research. *Qualitative Inquiry*, 5(1), 24–46.

Goodley, D. (2001). 'Learning Difficulties', the Social Model of Disability and Impairment: Challenging Epistemologies. *Disability & Society*, 16(2), 207–31.

Goodley, D. (2011). *Disability Studies: An Interdisciplinary Introduction*. London: SAGE Publications Ltd.

Goodley, D. and Roets, G. (2008). The (Be)comings and Goings of 'Developmental Disabilities': The Cultural Politics of 'Impairment'. *Discourse: Studies in the Cultural Politics of Education*, 29(2), 239–55.

Goodley, D. and Runswick-Cole, K. (2010). Emancipating Play: Dis/abled Children, Development and Deconstruction. *Disability & Society*, 25(4), 499–512.

Goodley, D. and Runswick-Cole, K. (2011a). Problematising Policy: Conceptions of 'Child', 'Disabled' and 'Parents' in Social Policy in England. *International Journal of Inclusive Education*, 15, 71–85.

Goodley, D. and Runswick-Cole, K. (2011b). The Violence of Disablism. *Sociology of Health & Illness*, 33(4), 602–17.

Goodley, D. and Runswick-Cole, K. (2012a). The Body as Disability and Possibility: Theorizing the 'Leaking, Lacking and Excessive' Bodies of Disabled Children. *Scandinavian Journal of Disability Research*, 1–19.

Goodley, D. and Runswick-Cole, K. (2012b). Reading Rosie: The Postmodern Disabled Child. *Education and Child Psychology*, 29(2), 53–66.

Goodley, D. and Runswick-Cole, K. (2012c, 19th December). *Resilience Life Story Phase Report*. Retrieved from http://disabilityresilience.wordpress.com/resilience-life-story-phase/ (accessed 16 July 2013).

Gordon, J. and Hollinger, V. (2002). *Edging into the Future: Science Fiction and Contemporary Cultural Transformation*. Philadelphia, PA: University of Pennsylvania Press.

Gordon, T. and Lahelma, E. (2002). Becoming an Adult: Possibilities and Limitations – Dreams and Fears. *Young*, 10(2), 2–18.

Greenstein, A. and Graby, S. (2013). *Supported Autonomy: Disability and Assistance beyond Modernism and Post-modernism*. Paper presented at the Theorising Normalcy and the Mundane 2013, Sheffield Hallam University. Retrieved from http://postpolitics101.wordpress.com/2013/09/27/supported-autonomy-disability-and-assistance-beyond-modernism-and-post-modernism/ (accessed 17 June 2014).

Guillemin, M. and Gillam, L. (2004). Ethics, Reflexivity, and 'Ethically Important Moments' in Research. *Qualitative Inquiry*, 10(2), 261–80.

Guinier, L. (1994). *The Tyranny of the Majority: Fundamental Fairness in Representative Democracy*. New York: Free Press.

Gunnarsson-Östling, U. (2011). Gender in Futures: A Study of Gender and Feminist Papers Published in Futures, 1969–2009. *Futures*, 43(9), 1029–39.

Halberstam, J. (1998). *Female Masculinity*. London: Duke University Press.

Hall, G.S. (1904). *Adolescence: Its Psychology and Its Relation to Physiology, Anthropology, Sociology, Sex, Crime, Religion and Education* (vols 1 and 2). New York: Appleton.

Hall, K.Q. (ed.) (2011). *Feminist Disability Studies*. Bloomington: Indiana University Press.

Hall, S. and Jefferson, T. (2006). Once More around Resistance through Rituals. In S. Hall and T. Jefferson (eds), *Resistance through Rituals: Youth Subcultures in Post-war Britain* (2nd edn). Oxon: Routledge, vii–xxxii.

Hansen, N. and Philo, C. (2007). The Normality of Doing Things Differently: Bodies, Spaces and Disability Geography. *Tijdschrift voor economische en sociale geografie*, 98(4), 493–506.

Haraldsdóttir, F. (2013). Simply Children. In T. Curran and K. Runswick-Cole (eds), *Disabled Children's Childhood Studies: Critical Approaches in a Global Context*. Basingstoke: Palgrave Macmillan, 13–21.

Haraldsdóttir, F. and Ágústsdóttir, E. (2012). *Hugmyndafræði NPA [The Principles of Independent Living]*. Paper presented at the Notendastýrð persónuleg aðstoð (NPA): Hugmyndafræði, framkvæmd, skipulag, samningar og fjármögnun notendastýrð persónuleg aðstoð [Independent Living (NPA): The concept, execution, planning, contracts and user-financing personal assistance], Reykjavik.

Haraldsdóttir, F. and Sigurðardttir, A. (eds). (2011). *Frjáls/Free*. Reykjavik: NPA Miðstöðin svf./The independent living centre in Iceland.

Haraway, D. (1988). Situated Knowledges: The Science Question in Feminism and the Privilege of Partial Perspective. *Feminist Studies*, 14(3), 575–99.

Hassouneh-Phillips, D. and McNeff, E. (2005). 'I Thought I was Less Worthy': Low Sexual and Body Esteem and Increased Vulnerability to Intimate Partner Abuse in Women with Physical Disabilities. *Sexuality and Disability*, 23(4), 227–40.

Heiss, S.N. (2011). Locating the Bodies of Women and Disability in Definitions of Beauty: An Analysis of Dove's Campaign for Real Beauty. *Disability Studies Quarterly*, 31(1). Retrieved from http://www.dsq-sds.org/article/view/1367/1497 (accessed 18 March 2012).

Hendey, N. and Pascall, G. (2002). *Becoming Adult: Young Disabled People Speak*. York: Joseph Rowntree Foundation.

Herndon, A. (2003). Disparate but Disabled: Fat Embodiment and Disability Studies. *NWSA Journal*, 14(3), 120–37.

Hicks, D. (2002). *Lessons for the Future: The Missing Dimension in Education*. London and New York: Routledge Falmer.

Hirst, M. and Baldwin, S. (1994). *Unequal Opportunities: Growing up Disabled*. London: HMSO.

Hodkinson, P. (2008). Youth Cultures: A Critical Outline of Key Debates. In P. Hodkinson and W. Deicke (eds), *Youth Cultures: Scences, Subcultures and Tribes*. Oxon: Routledge.

Holman Jones, S. and Adams, T.E. (2010). Autoethnography is a Queer Method. In K. Browne and C. Nash (eds), *Queer Methods and Methodologies: Intersecting Queer Theories and Social Science Research*. Farnham: Ashgate, 195–214.

hooks, b. (1982). *Ain't I a Woman: Black Women and Feminism*. London: Pluto.

hooks, b. (1994a). *Teaching to Transgress: Education as the Practice of Freedom*. London: Routledge.

hooks, b. (1994b). Theory as Liberatory Practice. *Teaching to Trangress: Education as the Practice of Freedom*. New York: Routlege, 59–75.

Horgan, G. (2003). Educable: Disabled Young People in Northern Ireland Challenge the Education System. In M. Shelvin and R. Rose (eds), *Encouraging Voice: Respecting the Insights of Young People Who Have Been Marginalised*. Dublin: The National Disability Authority, 100–120.

Horn, S.S. (2007). Adolescents' Acceptance of Same-Sex Peers Based on Sexual Orientation and Gender Expression. *Journal of Youth and Adolescence*, 36(3), 363–71.

Hornby, A.S. (ed.) (2010). *Oxford Advanced Learner's Dictionary* (8th edn, vol. 1). Oxford: Oxford University Press.

Hughes, B. (2001). Disability and the Constitution of Dependency. In L. Barton (ed.), *Disability, Politics and the Struggle for Change*. London: David Fulton Publishers, 24–33.

Hughes, B. (2005). What Can a Foucauldian Analysis Contribute to Disability Theory? In S. Tremain (ed.), *Foucault and the Government of Disability*. Michigan: University of Michigan Press, 78–92.

Hughes, B., Goodley, D. and Davis, L.J. (2012). Conclusion: Disability and Social Theory. In D. Goodley, B. Hughes and L.J. Davis (eds), *Disability and Social Theory: New Development and Directions*. Basingstoke: Palgrave Macmillan, 308–18.

Hughes, B., McKie, L., Hopkins, D. and Watson, N. (2005). Love's Labours Lost? Feminism, the Disabled People's Movement and an Ethic of Care. *Sociology*, 39(2), 259–75.

Hughes, B. and Paterson, K. (1997). The Social Model of Disability and the Disappearing Body: Towards a Sociology of Impairment. *Disability & Society*, 12(3), 325–40.

Hughes, B., Russell, R. and Paterson, K. (2005). Nothing to Be Had 'Off the Peg': Consumption, Identity and the Immobilization of Young Disabled People. *Disability & Society*, 20(1), 3–17.

Jaggar, A.M. (1989). Love and Knowledge: Emotion in Feminist Epistemology. *Inquiry*, 32(2), 151–76.

James, A. (2000). Embodied Being(s): Understanding the Self and the Body in Childhood. In A. Prout (ed.), *The Body, Childhood and Society*. Basingstoke: Macmillian Press Ltd., 19–37.

Josselson, R. (1996). On Writing Other People's Lives. In R. Josselson (ed.), *Ethics and Process in The Narrative Study of Lives*. California: Sage Publications.

July, G. (2014, 11th March). *Jealousy and Gender in Poly Relationships*. Retrieved from http://geojuly.blogspot.co.uk/ (accessed 15 May 2014).

Kafer, A. (2011). Debating Feminist Futures: Slippery Slopes, Cultural Anxiety, and the Case of the Deaf Lesbians. In K. Hall (ed.), *Feminist Disability Studies*. Bloomington: Indiana University Press, 218–42.

Kafer, A. (2013). *Feminist, Queer, Crip*. Bloomington: Indiana University Press.

Keay, D. (1987, 23rd September). No Such Thing as Society. *Woman's Own*.

Kelly, P. (2006). The Entrepreneurial Self and 'Youth at-Risk': Exploring the Horizons of Identity in the Twenty-first Century. *Journal of Youth Studies*, 9(1), 17–32.

Kelm, J.F. (2009). *Intellectual Disability and the Interdependent Expression of Self-Determination*. Interdisciplinary Master's Program in Disability Studies Master of Arts, The University of Manitoba, Winnipeg. Retrieved from http://www.collectionscanada.gc.ca/obj/thesescanada/vol2/002/MR63898.PDF (accessed 5 February 2011).

Kenyon, P. (Writer). (2011). Undercover Care: The Abuse Exposed [Television Documentary], *Panorama*. UK: BBC.

Kim, E. (2011). Asexuality in Disability Narratives. *Sexualities*, 14(4), 479–93.

Kittay, E.F. (1999). *Love's Labor: Essays on Women, Equality, and Dependency*. New York: Routledge.

Kittay, E.F. and Carlson, L. (eds) (2010). *Cognitive Disability and its Challenge to Moral Philosophy*. Oxford: Wiley-Blackwell.

Kleinsasser, A.M. (2000). Researchers, Reflexivity, and Good Data: Writing to Unlearn. *Theory into Practice*, 39(3), 155–62.

Kröger, T. (2009). Care Research and Disability Studies: Nothing in Common? *Critical Social Policy*, 29(3), 398–420.

Ladson Billings, G. (2011). Boyz to Men? Teaching to Restore Black Boys' Childhood. *Race Ethnicity and Education*, 14(1), 7–15.

Lahelma, E. and Gordon, T. (2008). Resources and (In(ter))dependence. *Young*, 16(2), 209–26.

Larner, W. (2003). Neoliberalism? *Environment and Planning D: Society and Space*, 21, 509–12.

Lavery, I., Knox, J. and Slevin, E. (1997). Learning Disabled People – The Forgotten Passengers? *Public Transport Planning and Operations*, 416, 141–52.

Lesko, N. (1996). Past, Present, and Future Conceptions of Adolescence. *Educational Theory*, 46(4), 453–72.

Lesko, N. (2002). Making Adolescence at the Turn of the Century: Discourse and the Exclusion of Girls. *Current Issues in Comparative Education*, 2(2), 182–90.

Lesko, N. (2012). *Act Your Age: A Cultural Construction of Adolescence* (2nd edn). New York and London: Routledge.

Levitas, R. (2005). *The Imaginary Reconstitution of Society or Why Sociologists and Others Should Take Utopia More Seriously*. Paper presented at the Inaugural Lecture, University of Bristol. Retrieved from http://www.bris.ac.uk/spais/files/inaugural.pdf (accessed 10 November 2014).

Liddiard, K. (2011). *(S)exploring Disability: Intimacies, Sexualities and Disabilities*. Doctor of Philosophy. Warwick: University of Warwick.

Liddiard, K. (2012). *Sex: Some Facts of Life*. Retrieved from http://www.disabilitynow.org.uk/living/up-close-personal/sex-some-facts-of-life?searchterm=kirsty (accessed 29 February 2012).

Little, J.A. (2006). *Feminist Philosophy and Science Fiction: Utopias and Dystopias*. Amherst, NY: Prometheus Books.

Löfgren-Mårtenson, L. (2013). 'Hip to be Crip?' About Crip Theory, Sexuality and People with Intellectual Disabilities. *Sexuality and Disability*, 31(4), 413–24.

Longmore, P.K. (2003). Why I Burned My Book. *Why I Burned My Book and Other Essays in Disability*. Philadelphia: Temple University Press, 230–59.

Lorde, A. (2007). Eye to Eye: Black Women, Hatred, and Anger. In A. Lorde (ed.), *Sister Ousider: Essays and Speeches by Audre Lorde*. Berkeley: Crossing Press (reprinted from: 1984), 145–75.

Lorde, A. (2012). *Sister Outsider: Essays and Speeches* (revised edn). New York: Random House Digital, Inc.

Mackenzie, C. and Stoljar, N. (2000a). Introduction: Autonomy Refigured. In C. Mackenzie and N. Stoljar (eds), *Relational Autonomy: Feminist Perspectives on Autonomy, Agency, and the Social Self*. New York: Oxford University Press, 3–34.

Mackenzie, C. and Stoljar, N. (eds) (2000b). *Relational Autonomy: Feminist Perspectives on Autonomy, Agency, and the Social Self*. New York: Oxford University Press.

Mallett, R. and Runswick-Cole, K. (2012). Commodifying Autism: The Cultural Contexts of 'Disability' in the Academy. In D. Goodley, B. Hughes and L. Davis (eds), *Disability and Social Theory: New Developments and Directions*. Basingstoke and New York: Palgrave MacMillan, 33–51.

Mallett, R. and Runswick-Cole, K. (2014). *Approaching Disability: Critical Issues and Perspectives*. London: Routledge.

Mallett, R. and Slater, J. (2014). Language. In C. Cameron (ed.), *Disability Studies: A Student's Guide*. London: Sage, 91–4.

Mathers, A. (2010). Road to Inclusion. *Learning Disability Today*, 10(9), 34–6.

McCarthy, M. (1998). Whose Body Is It Anyway? Pressures and Control for Women with Learning Disabilities. *Disability & Society*, 13(4), 557–74.

McLaughlin, J. (2006). Conceptualising Intensive Caring Activities: The Changing Lives of Families with Young Disabled Children. *Sociological Research Online*, 11(1).

McRobbie, A. (1980). Settling Accounts with Subcultures: A Feminist Critique. *Screen Education*, 34(Spring), 37–49.

McRobbie, A. (1990). *Feminism and Youth Culture*. London: Routledge.

McRobbie, A. (2000). The Culture of Working Class Girls. In A. McRobbie (ed.), *Feminism and Youth Culture* (2nd edn). London: Macmillan Press Ltd., 44–66. Retrieved from http://www.gold.ac.uk/media/working-class-girls. pdf (1977) (accessed 16 April 2011).

McRobbie, A. (2005). *The Uses of Cultural Studies: A Textbook*. London: SAGE.

McRobbie, A. and Garber, J. (2000). Girls and Subcultures. In A. McRobbie (ed.), *Feminism and Youth Culture* (2nd edn). London: Macmillan Press Ltd., 12–25.

McRuer, R. (2006a). Compulsory Able-Bodiedness and Queer/Disabled Existence. In L.J. Davis (ed.), *The Disability Studies Reader*. New York: Routledge, 369–81.

McRuer, R. (2006b). *Crip Theory*. New York: New York University Press.

Michalko, R. (2010). What's Cool About Blindness? *Disability Studies Quarterly*, 30(3/4). Retrieved from http://www.dsq-sds.org/article/view/1296/1332 (accessed 10 November 2014).

Mills, M. and Keddie, A. (2007). Teaching Boys and Gender Justice. *International Journal of Inclusive Education*, 11(3), 335–54.

Milojević, I. (2008). Timing Feminism, Feminising Time. *Futures*, 40(4), 329–45.

Mingus, M. (2011, 22nd August). *Moving Toward the Ugly: A Politic Beyond Desirability*. Retrieved from http://leavingevidence.wordpress. com/2011/08/22/moving-toward-the-ugly-a-politic-beyond-desirability/ (accessed 8 November 2014).

Mollow, A. (2012). Is Sex Disability? In R. McRuer and A. Mollow (eds), *Sex and Disability*. Durham and London: Duke University Press, 285–312.

More, T. (1972). *Utopia*. London: Folio Society.

Morris, J. (1991). *Pride against Prejudice: Transforming Attitudes to Disability*. Philidelphia: New Society Publishers.

Morris, J. (1992). Personal and Political: A Feminist Perspective on Researching Physical Disability. *Disability, Handicap & Society*, 7(2), 157–66.

Morris, J. (1997). Care of Empowerment? A Disability Rights Perspective. *Social Policy and Administration*, 31(1), 54–60.

Morris, J. (1998). *Feminist, Gender and Disability*. Leeds Disability Archive. Retrieved from http://www.leeds.ac.uk/disability-studies/archiveuk/ morris/gender%20and%20disability.pdf (accessed 24 February 2011).

Morris, J. (1999). *Move On Up: Supporting Young Disabled People in Their Transition to Adulthood.* Essex: Barnardo's.

Morris, J. (2002). *Young Disabled People Moving into Adulthood Foundations: Analysis Informing Change.* York: Joseph Rowntree Foundation.

Morss, J.R. (1996). *Growing Critical: Alternatives to Developmental Psychology.* London: Routledge.

Mudie, K. (2013, 19th January). Loads of Room to Talk! Bedroom Tax Tory Lord Freud Lives in Eight-bedroom Country Mansion. *Mirror.* Retrieved from http://www.mirror.co.uk/news/uk-news/bedroom-tax-tory-lord-freud -1545677 (accessed 7 June 2014).

Murray, P. (2002). *Hello! Are You Listening? Disabled Teenagers' Experiences of Access to Inclusive Leisure.* York: Joseph Rowntree Foundation.

Nagl-Docekal, H. (1999). The Feminist Critique of Reason Revisited. *Hypatia*, 14(1), 49–76.

Ndopu, E. (2013). *A Black Crip's Perspective on Fashion and Embodied Resistance.* Retrieved from http://thefeministwire.com/2013/02/a-black-crips-perspective-on-fashion-and-embodied-resistance/ (accessed 5 March 2014).

NPA Miðstöðin. (2013). *NPA Miðstöðin.* Retrieved from http://www.npa.is/ (accessed 15 September 2013).

Oakley, A. (1981). Interviewing Women: A Contradiction in Terms. In H. Roberts (ed.), *Doing Feminist Research.* London: Routledge & Kegan Paul plc., 30–62.

Oliver, M. (1990). *The Politics of Disablement.* London: Macmillan Education.

Overboe, J. (2007). Disability and Genetics: Affirming the Bare Life (The State of Exception). *Canadian Review of Sociology/Revue canadienne de sociologie*, 44(2), 219–35.

Owen, R. and Harris, S.P. (2012). 'No Rights without Responsibilities': Disability Rights and Neoliberal Reform under New Labour. *Disability Studies Quarterly*, 32(3). Retrieved from http://dsq-sds.org/article/view/3283/3110 (accessed 28 October 2013).

Oxford Online Dictionary. (2013). Independent. Retrieved from http://www.oxforddictionaries.com/definition/english/independent (accessed 13 December 2013).

Payne, E. and Smith, M. (2012). Rethinking Safe Schools Approaches for LGBTQ Students: Changing the Questions We Ask. *Multicultural Perspectives*, 14(4), 187–93.

Payne, M.A. (2010). Teen Brain Science and the Contemporary Storying of Psychological (Im)maturity. In H. Blatterer and J. Glahn (eds), *Times of Our Lives: Making Sense of: Growing Up and Growing Old.* Oxford: Inter-disciplinary Press, 55–68.

Peck, J. and Tickell, A. (2002). Neoliberalizing Space. *Antipode*, 34(3), 380–404.

Pidd, H. (2013, 25th March). Youth Clubs Shut Down as Councils Slash Spending on Their Future. *The Guardian*. Retrieved from http://www.theguardian.com/society/2013/mar/25/drime-focus-youth-services-cuts (accessed 14 December 2013).

Pillow, W. (2003). Confession, Catharsis, or Cure? Rethinking the Uses of Reflexivity as Methodological Power in Qualitative Research. *International Journal of Qualitative Studies in Education*, 16(2), 175–96.

Priestley, M. (2003). *Disability: A Life Course Approach*. Cambridge: Bridge Press.

Rabiee, P., Priestley, M. and Knowles, J. (2001). *Whatever Next? Young Disabled People Leaving Care*. Leeds: First Key.

Rattansi, A. and Phoenix, A. (2005). Rethinking Youth Identities: Modernist and Postmodernist Frameworks. *Identity*, 5(2), 97–123.

Reeve, D. (2002). Negotiating Psycho-emotional Dimensions of Disability and Their Influence on Identity Constructions. *Disability & Society*, 17(5), 493–508.

Reeve, D. (2012). *Part of the Problem or Part of the Solution? A Discussion of the Reality of 'Inclusive Access for Disabled Customers'*. Paper presented at the Disability – Spaces and Places of Exclusion Symposium, Lancaster University.

Richardson, L. (1998). Writing: A Method of Inquiry. In N.K. Denzin and Y.S. Lincoln (eds), *Collecting and Interpreting Qualitative Materials*. London: SAGE Publications, Ltd., 345–72.

Robinson, K. (2008). In the Name of 'Childhood Innocence': A Discursive Exploration of the Moral Panic Associated with Childhood and Sexuality. *Cultural Studies Review*, 14(2), 113–29.

Roets, G., Adams, M. and Hove, G.V. (2006). Challenging the Monologue about Silent Sterilization: Implications for Self-advocacy. *British Journal of Learning Disabilities*, 34(3), 167–74.

Roets, G. and Goedgeluck, M. (2007). Daisies on the Road. *Qualitative Inquiry*, 13(1), 85–112.

Rothblum, E. and Soloway, S. (eds) (2009). *The Fat Studies Reader*. New York and London: New York University Press.

Roulstone, A. and Prideaux, S. (2011). *Understanding Disability Policy*. Bristol: Policy Press.

Rouse, J. (2007). Power/Knowledge. In G. Gutting (ed.), *The Cambridge Companion to Foucault* (2nd edn). New York: Cambridge University Press, 95–122.

Rousso, H. (2013). *Don't Call Me Inspirational: A Disabled Feminist Talks Back*. Philadelphia: Temple University Press.

Runswick-Cole, K. and Goodley, D. (2011). Big Society: A Dismodernist Critique. *Disability & Society*, 26(7), 881–5.

Runswick-Cole, K. and Goodley, D. (2013). Resilience: A Disability Studies and Community Psychology Approach. *Social and Personality Psychology Compass*, 7(2), 67–78.

Russell, M. (1998). *Beyond Ramps: Disability at the End of the Social Contract: A Warning from an Uppity Crip*. Monroe: Common Courage Press.

Ryan, S. and Runswick-Cole, K. (2008). Repositioning Mothers: Mothers, Disabled Children and Disability Studies. *Disability & Society*, 23(3), 199–210.

Sandahl, C. (1999). Ahhhh Freak Out! Metaphors of Disability and Femaleness in Performance. *Theatre Topics*, 9(1), 11–30.

Sargisson, L. (2000). *Utopian Bodies and the Politics of Transgression*. London: Routledge.

Schwandt, T.A. (1997). *Qualitative Inquiry: A Dictionary of Terms*. California: Sage Publications.

Scott, J. and Marshall, G. (2009). *Oxford Dictionary of Sociology* (3rd edn). Oxford: Oxford University Press.

Sedgwick, E.K. (1990). *Epistemology of the Closet*. Berkeley: University of California Press.

Shakespeare, T. (2006). *Disability Rights and Wrongs*. Oxon: Routledge.

Shakespeare, T. and Watson, N. (2001). The Social Model of Disability: An Outdated Ideology? Exploring Theories and Expanding Methodologies. *Research in Social Science and Disability*, 2, 9–28.

Sharma, N. (2002). *Still Missing Out? Ending Poverty and Social Exclusion: Messages to Government from Families with Disabled Children*. Basildon: Barnardo's.

Sheppard, E. (2014). *Crippling Pain: Examining Pain in Discourses of Normal Human Experience*. Paper presented at the Theorising Normalcy and the Mundane: More Questions of the Human, University of Sheffield.

Sherry, M. (2004). Overlaps and Contradictions between Queer Theory and Disability Studies. *Disability & Society*, 19(7), 769–83.

Shildrick, M. (1997). *Leaky Bodies and Boundaries: Feminism, Postmodernism and (Bio)ethics*. London and New York: Routledge.

Shildrick, M. (2004). Performativity: Disability after Deleuze. *Scan: Journal of Media Arts Culture*, 1(3). Retrieved from http://www.scan.net.au/scan/journal/display.php?journal_id=36 (accessed 10 November 2014).

Shildrick, M. (2009). *Dangerous Discourses of Disability, Subjectivity and Sexuality*. New York: Palgrave Macmillan.

Skjaldardóttir, S.S. (2012, 17th Feburary). *Fötluð lesbía, er það til?* [Disabled Lesbians, is There Such a Thing?]. Retrieved from http://www.innihald.is/index.php/thjodfelagsmal/mannrettindi/item/754-foetludh-lesbia-er-thadh-til (accessed 18 February 2012).

Slater, J. (2012a). Stepping Outside Normative Neoliberal Discourse: Youth and Disability Meet – The Case of Jody McIntyre. *Disability & Society*, 27(5), 723–7.

Slater, J. (2012b). Youth for Sale: Using Critical Disability Perspectives to Examine the Embodiment of 'Youth'. *Societies*, 2(3), 195–209.

Slater, J. (2013a). Playing Grown-up: Using Critical Disability Perspectives to Rethink Youth. In A. Azzopardi (ed.), *Youth: Responding to Lives – An International Handbook*. Rotterdam: Sense Publications, 75–92.

Slater, J. (2013b). Research with Dis/abled Youth: Taking a Critical Disability, 'Critically Young' Positionality. In K. Runswick-Cole and T. Curran (eds), *Disabled Children's Childhood Studies: Critical Approaches in a Global Context*. Basingstoke: Palgrave.

Slater, J. (f.c.-a). The (Normal) Non-normativity of Youth. In R. Mallett, C.A. Ogden and J. Slater (eds), *Theorising Normalcy and The Mundane: Precarious Positions*. Chester: Chester University Press.

Slater, J. (f.c.-b). Stresses and Contradictions of 'Doing Feminisms' in the (Neo)liberal Academy. *Feminism & Psychology*.

Slater, J., Ágústsdóttir, E. and Haraldsdóttir, F. (2012). *Queering Adulthood: Three Stories of Growing Up*. Paper presented at the Child, Youth, Family and Disability Conference, Manchester Metropolitan University.

Sloan, J. (2010, 12 August). Help Us Stop 1.5bn Benefits Scroungers, *The Sun*. Retrieved from http://www.thesun.co.uk/sol/homepage/features/3091717/The-Sun-declares-war-on-Britains-benefits-culture.html (accessed 16 March 2011).

Smith, C. (2014, 5th March). *Normcore is Bullsh*t*. Retrieved from http://www.thestylecon.com/2014/03/03/normcore-bullsht/ (accessed 18 April 2014).

Smith, M. (2011). Young People and the 2011 'Riots' in England – Experiences, Explanations and Implications for Youth Work. *The Encyclopedia of Informal Education*. Retrieved from http://www.infed.org/archives/jeffs_and_smith/young_people_youth_work_and_the_2011_riots_in_england.html (accessed 18 November 2011).

Sothern, M. (2007). You Could Truly be Yourself if You Just Weren't You: Sexuality, Disabled Body Space, and the (Neo)liberal Politics of Self-help. *Environment and Planning D: Society and Space*, 25(1), 144–59.

Sparkes, A.C. (2002). Autoethnography: Self-Indulgence or Something More? In A.P. Bochner and C. Ellis (eds), *Ethnographically Speaking: Autoethnography, Literature, and Aesthetics*. Walnut Creek and Oxford: AltraMira Press, 209–32.

Spry, T. (2001). Performing Autoethnography: An Embodied Methodological Praxis. *Qualitative Inquiry*, 7(6), 706–32.

Stainton, T. (2001). Reason and Value: The Thought of Plato and Aristotle and the Construction of Intellectual Disability. *Mental Retardation*, 39(6), 452–60.

Stein, I. (2010). Breaking a Disabled Limb: Social and Medical Construction of 'Legitimate' and 'Illegitimate' Impairments. *Disability Studies Quarterly*, 30(3/4). Retrieved from http://www.dsq-sds.org/article/view/1294/1330 (accessed 11 November 2014).

Stonewall. (2010). *Legal Equality in the UK.* Retrieved from http://www.youngstonewall.org.uk/know_your_rights/legal_equality_in_the_uk/ (accessed 16 July 2014).

Stratton, A. (2011, 15th August). David Cameron on Riots: Broken Society is Top of My Political Agenda, *The Guardian.* Retrieved from http://www.theguardian.com/uk/2011/aug/15/david-cameron-riots-broken-society (accessed 4 July 2014).

Sullivan, A. (2004). *Same-Sex Marriage: Pro and Con.* London: Vintage.

Tengström, A. (no date). *Presentation of JAG.* Retrieved from http://www.independentliving.org/docs5/jag.html (accessed 29 March 2012).

Thomas, C. (1999). *Female Forms: Experiencing and Understanding Disability.* Buckingham: Open University Press.

Thomas, C. (1999). *Female Forms: Experiencing and Understanding Disability.* Buckingham: Open University Press.

Tilley, E., Walmsley, J., Earle, S. and Atkinson, D. (2012). 'The Silence is Roaring': Sterilization, Reproductive Rights and Women with Intellectual Disabilities. *Disability & Society,* 27(3), 413–26.

Tillmann-Healy, L.M. (2003). Friendship as Method. *Qualitative Inquiry,* 9(5), 729–49.

Timimi, S., Gardner, N. and McCabe, B. (2010). *The Myth of Autism: Medicalising Men's and Boys' Social and Emotional Competence.* Basingstoke: Palgrave Macmillan.

Titchkosky, T. (2000). Disability Studies: The Old and the New. *Canadian Journal of Sociology,* 25(2), 197–224.

Titchkosky, T. (2003). Governing Embodiment: Technologies of Constituting Citizens with Disabilities. *Canadian Journal of Sociology,* 28(4), 517–42.

Titchkosky, T. (2007). *Reading and Writing Disability Differently: The Textured Life of Embodiment.* Toronto: University of Toronto Press.

Titchkosky, T. (2010). The Not-Yet-Time of Disability in the Bureaucratization of University Life. *Disability Studies Quarterly,* 30(3/4). Retrieved from http://www.dsq-sds.org/article/view/1295/1331 (accessed 11 November 2014).

Titchkosky, T. (2011). *The Question of Access: Disability, Space, Meaning.* Toronto and London: University of Toronto Press.

Titchkosky, T. (2012). *Disability and the Poverty of Imagination in Neo-liberal Times.* Paper presented at the Disability Studies Conference, Lancaster University.

Tøssebro, J. (2004). Introduction to the Special Issue: Understanding Disability. *Scandinavian Journal of Disability Research,* 2(1), 3–7.

Tregaskis, C. (2004). *Constructions of Disability: Researching the Interface between Disabled and Non-disabled People.* London: Routledge.

Tregaskis, C. and Goodley, D. (2005). Disability Research by Disabled and Non-Disabled People: Towards a Relational Methodology of Research Production. *International Journal of Social Research Methodology,* 8(5), 363–74.

Tremain, S. (2006). Reproductive Freedom, Self-regulation, and the Government of Impairment in Utero. *Hypatia*, 21(1), 35–53.

Veck, W. (2002). Completing the Story: Connecting Relational and Psychological Processes of Exclusion. *Disability & Society*, 17(5), 529–40.

Waite, J. (2013). *To What Extent Do Public Libraries in the UK Provide Adequate Resources for Trans People?* A study submitted in partial fulfilment of the requirements for the degree of Master of Arts in Librarianship. Sheffield iSchool. The University of Sheffield. Sheffield.

Walkerdine, V. (1993). Beyond Developmentalism? *Theory & Psychology*, 3(4), 451–69.

Walmsley, J. (1993). Contradictions in Caring: Reciprocity and Interdependence. *Disability, Handicap & Society*, 8(2), 129–41.

Walmsley, J. (2001). Normalisation, Emancipatory Research and Inclusive Research in Learning Disability. *Disability & Society*, 16(2), 187–205.

Ware, L. (2005). Many Possible Futures, Many Different Directions: Merging Critical Special Education and Disability Studies. In S. Gabel (ed.), *Disability Studies in Education: Readings in Theory and Method*. New York: Peter Lang Publishing, 103–24.

Warner, M. (2003). *The Trouble with Normal: Sex, Politics, and the Ethics of Queer Life*. Cambridge, Massachusetts: Harvard University Press.

Watson, N. (2002). Well, I Know this is Going to Sound Very Strange to You, But I Don't See Myself as a Disabled Person: Identity and Disability. *Disability & Society*, 17(5), 509–27.

Watson, N., Shakespeare, T., Cunningham-Burley, S., Barnes, C., Corker, M., Davis, J. and Priestley, M. (1999). *Life as a Disabled Child: A Qualitative Study of Young People's Experiences and Perspectives*. The University of Leeds.

Watt, D. (2007). On Becoming a Qualitative Researcher: The Value of Reflexivity. *The Qualitative Report*, 12(1), 82–101.

Watts, I.E. and Erevelles, N. (2004). These Deadly Times: Reconceptualizing School Violence by Using Critical Race Theory and Disability Studies. *American Educational Research Journal*, 41(2), 271–99.

Wendell, S. (2010). Toward a Feminist Theory of Disability. In L.J. Davis (ed.), *The Disability Studies Reader* (3rd edn). New York and London: Routledge, 336–52.

Wickenden, M. (2010). *Teenage Worlds, Different Voices: An Ethnographic Study of Identity and the Lifeworlds of Disabled Teenagers who use AAC*. Doctoral Thesis, The University of Sheffield. Retrieved from http://etheses.whiterose. ac.uk/860/2/wickenden_final_thesis.pdf (accessed 16 January 2012).

Willis, P. (1977). *Learning to Labour: How Working Class Kids Get Working Class Jobs*. Farnborough: Saxon House.

Wilson, L.-M. (2003). *An Overview of the Literature on Disability and Transport*. London: Disability Rights Commission.

Wyn, J. and White, R. (2000). Negotiating Social Change. *Youth & Society*, 32(2), 165–83.

Yates, S. and Roulstone, A. (2012). Social Policy and Transitions to Training and Work for Disabled Young People in the United Kingdom: Neo-liberalism for Better and for Worse? *Disability & Society*, 28(4), 456–70.

Zukas, H. (1975). *The History of the Berkeley Center for Independent Living (CIL)*. Paper presented at the Report of the State of the Art Conference, Center for Independent Living, Berkeley, California. Retrieved from http://www.independentliving.org/docs3/zukas.html (accessed 11 November 2014).

Index

Page numbers in **bold** indicate a figure. Numbers followed by 'n' refer to footnotes.

DATE DUE	RETURNED